MY WITNESS OF JESUS

By: Katherine E. Hether

Printed in the United States of America

Raintree Press, LLC
12180 South 300 East
Suite 1238
Draper, Utah 84020

www.raintreepress.com

MY WITNESS OF JESUS

By: Katherine E. Hether

This book is dedicated to my Christian husband James, and the many mentors God has placed from season to season throughout my life thus far, with more to come before my days upon the earth are fulfilled. (Haggai 2:9) "And the glory of your latter days will be greater than the former, and in this place, you will have peace."

My Witness of Jesus
Copyright applied for:
Library of Congress Control # applied for
ISBN # 978-0-9993363-8-0

www.katherinehether.com

Content

Introduction

This book is not meant as an autobiography of my life by any means. But rather an accounting of the many encounters with Jesus Christ throughout my life thus far. After reading this, my prayer is that you will take time to reflect on your encounters with Jesus in your life. Then let your light shine by sharing your own witness of Christ to others.

Revelations 12:11 "And they overcame him (Satan) by the Blood of the Lamb and by the word of their testimony."

I have heard many times that 'Light' is one of God's weapons for spreading His goodness. Matthew 5:16 "In the same way, let your light shine before others, that they may see your good deeds and glorify your Father in Heaven."

Here you will read a true accounting of God's goodness that I have encountered. 1 Samuel 17:34-35 But David said to Saul, "Your servant used to keep sheep for his father; and when there came a lion, or a bear, and took a lamb from the flock, I went after him and struck him and delivered it out of his mouth; and if he arose against me, I caught him by his beard, and struck him and killed him."

In Biblical Times men always carried a staff to walk the rocky terrain, and ward off wild animals. Most importantly, they used their staff to record special events in their lives. One example of this is when God delivered them out of harm, they would carve notches in the staff to remind them. Each notch on the staff in order from top to bottom told their story.

In today's literary writings these notches would be called snippets. This book shares snippets of my special faith and belief in God, and so my journey with the Lord begins...

Chapter One

Listening When God Calls You

I've sat down several times as a Christian writer wanting to share my witness of the many encounters I've had with The Lord. But work deadlines on a Christian Romance/Mystery Series took precedence. In between the last two books of the series, two Fictional/Religious Books for Christmas and Easter 'fell into my head' when I sat down at the keyboard. So, I had to work on them. After those were published, the outline of the fourth novel, Project Isaiah, called to me after watching the news one evening about a subject that should have been eradicated in the United States years ago. Human Trafficking still rages in America and throughout the world by an intermingled network of Globalist. By the way, each book is totally fictitious consisting of a mixture of fiction with real life situations.

It is by no mistake that the Christian Romance/Mystery Series was inspired by God. It started out by attending an Apparition of Mary in Conyers, Georgia in the late 1980's. At that time, being the mother of a large family, I saw the decaying of our society transforming from the Culture of Life that God intended into a Culture of Death void of God.

The very first time I attended the Apparition an idea for a book addressing this subject to teenagers' sort of 'fell into my head.' On the way home, ideas for the characters and storyline seemed to jump out at me. The next morning after I got the last of the children on the school bus, I was busy at my computer beginning a book that soon turned into a series.

It wasn't until years later during a camping trip to Bear Lake on the Utah/Idaho Border, while sitting around a family campfire late, one night watching the massive stars in the sky, God's promise to Abraham popped into my mind. Genesis 15:5 "And He (God) brought him (Abraham) outside and said, 'Look toward heaven, and the number of stars,'" Then He said to him, "So shall your descendants be."

Later, falling asleep in the camper staring out a small window I was mesmerized watching multiple, shooting stars. Somehow, that triggered the times God intervened in my life. I felt very strongly that God was calling me to share my witness of Christ.

But before I begin sharing my great journey with Christ, I must confess that throughout my life, it hasn't always been a bed of roses but far from it! John 16:33 "I have told you these things, so that in Me you may have peace. In this world you will have trouble but take heart! I have overcome the world." And also, in Luke 12:48 "For unto whomsoever much is given, of him shall be much required."

In a way, these two scriptures sum up the painful agony intermixed with the greatest moments of ecstasy to date in my life. The stark contrast of walking with Christ in the Light to traveling through the darkest depths of Hell to save some of my children, and family members was on a road I never knew existed, nor did I ever want to tread. Instead, I was forced on roads that took my loving Christian heart and tore it apart.

The only thing that pulled me through those agonizing circumstances was Jesus carrying me. Fr. M.J. Joachim Tierney, a Monk in Conyers, Georgia taught me that the Scriptures are a Blueprint for surviving this world. He warned that partaking of the Eucharist as often as possible is the only thing that will keep us steadfast until the end.

Fr. Tierney shared his devotion to Mother Mary with me to lead me through the trials of motherhood. Mary too faced heart wrenching trials with her Son, Jesus Christ from His conception, His Death on the Cross, and Resurrection. The sacrifice Jesus willingly paid for all mankind to return to the Father.

Fr. Tierney had me turn to the Book of Luke 2:25-35. The Prophecy of Simeon's words in the Temple when Mary and Joseph obediently took Baby Jesus to consecrate Him to the Lord. Jesus was just forty days old when Simeon's words to fulfill the requirement of the Law of Moses to Mary, foreshadowed the very suffering that Jesus would ultimately endure, stating, "a sword will pierce your own soul also."

It is evident that Mary suffered on the cross with Jesus far beyond any mortal mother. The sculpture, The Madonna Della Pieta carved by Michelangelo represents the "sixth sorrow" of the Virgin Mary that Simeon prophesied. It is enshrined in St. Peter's Basilica in the Vatican City.

The suffering of Mary watching the Romans crucifying her Son is unfathomable to comprehend. Yet the scriptures only touch a small portion of the Life of Christ. But Mary witnessed His entire life, including all the miracles He performed maturing as the Son of God.

It is through Mary that we learn of His miraculous conception and birth, her and Joseph finding Jesus at age twelve in the Temple talking with the Jewish ruling class, consisting of Nicodemus a High Priest of the Sadducees, the Pharisees, and Scribes. The Child they kept hidden, suddenly emerged on His own, to the very people Simeon warned Mary about.

It was in Cana that Mary showed her knowledge of Jesus' Heavenly presence upon the Earth. In Jewish customs running out of wine would have publicly shamed Mary's family. When Jesus and His followers joined Mary at her cousin's wedding, she said, "they have no wine." Jesus questioned Mary for wanting Him to get involved with her cousin's wedding, since He hadn't begun His public ministry.

But also in Jewish customs, Mothers were counselors. So, by Jesus' questioning Mary in effect, He meant this would begin His way to the Passion. Mary's answer was twofold. She knew that His newfound followers needed to witness Jesus performing a miracle. Thomas worked for the company providing the wine. Thomas knew there wasn't enough wine and watered it down to make it last throughout the ceremony. By Thomas witnessing this profound miracle, he left everything to follow Jesus.

Secondly, Mary knew Jesus was ready to begin His way to the Passion. She approved by telling the servants, "Do whatever He tells you."

Chapter 2

My Destiny Unfolds

My first encounter with the Lord's protection began with an abusive relative approaching me at age nine-years-old and told me not to tell or I would be hurt. The Holy Spirit warned me of how horribly wrong the request was, and I fled to my mother's side afraid to say anything.

And again, at age thirteen-years-old, I found myself forced to stay outside my house during a Florida thunderstorm with sharp lightning striking all around me. We both knew our mother and sister would be gone when we got home from school. I worried all the way home on the bus about the bad weather and getting inside my locked bedroom, before he arrived.

He drove his car, and the bus was late. So, by the time I got into our back yard, he was already on the back porch taunting me to come inside. He laughed while watching me stand under the trees flinching and screaming with fear from lightning strikes. I'll never forget crying out to God to protect me from getting struck and from him.

At that moment God heard my cries, protecting me from the storm and gave me the special gift of The Holy Spirit to always sense very strongly when I was alone, and he was nearby.

I knew then that God's love is infinite, overflowing to those who seek Him. Psalms 20:1 "May the Lord answer you when you are in distress; may the Name of the God of Jacob protect you." Needless to say, I spent most of my childhood avoiding him. Throughout my marriage and while raising

9

children, I ensured that I was never alone in his presence. After he died, I found out from another family member that I was the first of a long line of many victims.

Hebrews 13:6 "I will never leave thee or forsake thee." This was just the beginning of The Holy Spirit protecting and helping me.

God Has Plans For Us

Little did I know that God had something already planned for my life. Backing up two years at age eleven, I was on the beach in Ormond with my older sister, Alma and her best friend, Claire. It so happened that Claire's mother needed to give her a message and sent her brother Eddie to find us. Eddie along with his friend found us near the beach approach by their home. It was during this brief conversation with Eddie and his friend where God's love and plan for my destiny would begin to unfold.

Jeremiah 29:11 "For I know the plans I have for you," declares the Lord, "plans to prosper you and not to harm you, plans to give you hope and a future."

God's Plan Begins To Unfold

Skipping ahead to a middle school dance located on City Island in Daytona by the Yacht Basin, God again foreshadowed my destiny.

Mainland High School's Football Coach ran the Youth Center on Friday nights. Since it was operated by the football coach that had coached my older brother, my father deemed it safe for me to attend. This particular evening it was Dad's turn to drop me and a friend off. As we walked toward the entrance, a girl in my science class ran out of the building after another girl and started to fight with her. Two boys hurried out behind them trying to break up the fight. One of the outside chaperones also tried to break it up but couldn't, so he called the police.

That's when I noticed one of the boys looked very familiar. He quickly grabbed my classmate by the hand, pulling her away from the fight. But he stopped for a second, turned around and stared directly at me, as if he recognized me too. Then, they ran to the Yacht Basin and jumped into a small boat. Rumor was the boys stole the boat and took off.

My friend and I hurried to the dock in time to watch them head across the Basin. We found out on Monday that the boys went to Seabreeze High School in Daytona Beach across the river. The funny thing is years later, little did I know that the boy that stared at me, and had 'stolen' the boat would have a major role in my life and so, my story continues . . .

A Father's Blessing

Two years later, our family was waiting on my sister to weigh her meat before she sat down. She was on a Weight Watcher's diet and Dad liked to rib her about it. This particular night, Dad was in a funny mood and out of the blue went around the table giving each child a blessing.

A Father's blessing is important, beginning clear back to The Old Testament. It was a very, serious blessing usually given to the firstborn son. It was not to be given lightly. But I will say that all of Dad's blessings, jokes or not, came true in our family. Mine was that I wouldn't finish college and run off with some guy.

It was shortly after that blessing, when I realized the boy on the beach in Ormond with my sister's friend was the same one that night at the City Island Dance. That's why he stared at me before running off to the Yacht Basin. I would soon realize that God used my father to foreshadow the way I would leave home with my future husband. The main lesson that I learned is that nothing with God is by chance or coincidence. As a matter of fact, now I always say, 'Coincidence is God's way of staying anonymous.'

Another Planned Coincidence

Soon after our Father's Blessing, I was by the kitchen phone one Saturday when it rang during lunch. I answered the call that would later concern my future mother-in-law. My father owned a small glass company, Atlas Glass, Inc. near our house in Port Orange.

The Ormond Beach Post Office was fifteen miles away from our house, but only a few streets from her house. My father was urgently needed to immediately board up the large, front plate-glass window. An elderly woman driving a new Cadillac pulled into the parking lot in front of the Post Office. Instead of stepping on the brake, she hit the gas, jumping the high curve, slamming through the window, pinning a customer against the counter, breaking both of the woman's legs.

Sunday morning, the accident made the front-page headlines of the Daytona Beach News Journal. I read the injured customer's name was Twila Hether. She was in the Post Office mailing a package to her newly, married son, Airman First Class, James E. Hether, stationed in Da Nang, Vietnam.

Ask God For Wisdom

My destiny wasn't fully manifested until two years later, on a Sunday morning when I was searching for the newspaper to read the cartoon strip of the week. My sister had just finished reading it and handed me the paper opened to the obituaries and divorces. As I skimmed through the paper while turning the page, a now familiar name jumped out at me. It was James E. Hether vs. Jennifer A. Hether.

James 1:5 "If any of you lacks wisdom, let him ask God, who gives to all men generously and without reproaching, and it will be given him."

It wasn't until I said a quick prayer that it came to me. The newspaper article of the woman in the Ormond Beach Post Office popped into my head. I remembered the article said she was mailing a package to her newly, married son stationed in Da Nang.

Recently, it had been all over the news about soldiers receiving 'Dear John' Letters while they were serving in the Vietnam War. I remembered feeling how sad that it happened to her son. She had recovered from two broken legs and now would have to help her son go through a divorce.

But what I didn't realize was that God was arranging our lives together in the background. I also had no clue how soon that name would appear to me again.

A few months later in December at Daytona Beach Community College, James Hether (Jim) pointed me out to a mutual friend and told him that he was going to marry me. Jeff told him my name and said that I was in one of his classes. He said that I was a classy chick and wouldn't have anything to do with him.

13

But that was not what God had planned for both of us, since we were young. Jim meant what he said about marrying me, so he found out from Jeff the times when I was in the Student Center. The next day, Jim found me and introduced himself. We had coffee together and started talking. We missed our next two classes talking as if we'd known each other our entire lives. He invited me to the nearby Steak and Shake for lunch. From that moment on it was absolutely love at first sight. We met every morning at the Student Center for coffee and he'd walk me to class. The engine in his VW Camper blew and was in the shop, so we never went out on an evening date, and my family never met Jim.

Chapter Three

A Strength From Within

The morning before Christmas break, Jim asked me to go to California with him. I knew my father would never approve of it. I'd never gone against either of my parents but without hesitation I felt deep down in my heart, it was the right thing God wanted me to do.

What I didn't know is that God already had a plan set in motion to handle my father. Early in the morning the day after Christmas, my mother received a phone call that her father was ill and in the hospital. My parents and younger brother quickly packed for Georgia. I had started a new job and couldn't go with them. What was odd, is that they never left me home alone overnight even though I had turned eighteen in October.

So, what would any eighteen-year-old do, especially since she got a set of red suitcases for Christmas? I hurried to the phone to call Jim; except he never gave me his phone number. I searched the now obsolete phonebook and called the first Hether in Ormond. Luckily, Jim answered the phone or I would have totally lost my nerve. Jim gladly picked me up a few hours later to begin our lives together. Looking back, we realized that God was guiding our every step towards our journey together.

Oh, and by the way, my grandfather recovered within a few days and my parents returned home only to find out from my sister that we had left to elope. Proverbs 6:2 "You are snared in the utterance of your lips, caught in the words of your mouth." My Father's blessing years earlier came to fruition.

I must add an interesting note about my Grandpa Irving William Hiers. I got my story telling ability from him. Since we were young children, every time we visited Grandpa, he would always sit in a kitchen chair next to the couch. He would take his hat off and sit it on the floor beside the chair. It was his rule that we were never allowed to touch that hat. He would begin a fantastic story but by the time he was almost finished, he'd start laughing so hard that we never heard any of the endings. I always wondered if it was by design, since he was winging the entire story. Did it really have an ending? So, as an author, I always make sure the path to the ending of the story is very clear. Sort of like another person in our family genealogy, Thomas Jefferson did when he wrote the Declaration of Independence.

Our Trip to California

Jim was honorably discharged for medical reasons; due to a herniated disk he received during a missile attack on the runway at Da Nang Air Force Base. He was standing on the runway when the rockets began to hit the tarmac coming straight for him. Running for his life, he climbed up the revetment wall around the airplane that he was working on when a rocket struck near him. The explosion threw him on the other side where he landed on his back. Badly injured, Jim was unable to stand or turn over and crawled into a nearby bunker for safety. Later, he finds out that sixty rockets in one minute struck the runway in a direct line to the airplane he was working on. God protected him.

After the rocket attack, he was so badly injured, they put him aboard a C-130 Hercules along with other injured soldiers on route to a hospital in Camron Bay. During the flight, three of the four engines were shot by enemy fire. The "Flying Brick" as it was called was able to make an emergency landing with only one engine. As the plane was landing, the pilot lowered the back of the plane, and the soldiers watched as firetrucks, and ambulances chase after the plane until it stopped. They were all ordered to evacuate the plane immediately.

I learned in the short time when Jim was in Vietnam; he was also the only survivor of an airplane crash in the jungle. He was in the enemies' hands, and the Marines rescued him along with a South Vietnamese Soldiers. The Marines took them to the nearest Chow Hall. In the middle of the night, they opened it for them. They ate like they hadn't eaten in a week.

After Jim's discharge, he qualified for the GI Bill to pay for his schooling. Hence, that's when I met Jim at Daytona Beach Jr. College. Jim was in pre-law, but God had a different plan for his career in the health field to help the injured.

But in the late 1960's, what would two young kids in love want to do? We decided to put school on hold and travel the country in his 1967 Volkswagen Camper. On our three-month travels from Florida to California, California to Pennsylvania, and Pennsylvania back to Daytona, we shared our beliefs in God stopping at Catholic Churches along the way. We also prayed before every meal and had a travel prayer before we traveled.

Our first stop was California. We were staying with old friends of his, who had lined up a job for Jim before we left Florida. We only stayed with them for three weeks. I never felt comfortable around them, especially the girl. She seemed to whisper a lot to Jim. The final straw was the last night we were there. Her husband insisted I go with him to get something for dinner. I instantly didn't feel right about it but was urged to go. He seemed to be taking his time getting home. The Holy Spirit was warning me that something was wrong. When I finally got back, I immediately told Jim what I felt. That's when he explained to me that we were staying with his ex-wife and her new husband. The uncomfortable feeling was The Holy Spirit warning me. I immediately wanted to leave-period! We packed and left.

That's when Jim got a better job offer from a friend's mother, who owned a fencing company in Pennsylvania. So, off we went back to the Northern East Coast to start his new job. We were supposed to stay at their house, except for Jim not telling his new boss about me. When we arrived at the house, she opened the door, and I was standing behind Jim. Behind his boss was her daughter about our age. She jumped out wearing an Easter Bunny Costume, complete with the long, pink, and white ears complimented by the fluffy, white tail. Needless to say, when Jim introduced me, the offer to stay at the house was immediately withdrawn. So, we went to his grandfather's house.

Misko Chockan's Unshakeable Faith

We stayed with his Grandfather, Michael Chakan, (Misko Chockan-Russian name) for a while. All the way to Pennsylvania Jim would tell me stories of his grandparents. As a young boy growing up in Sid Austria-Hungary, Grandpa spoke seven languages fluently. He worked as an interpreter for the Russian Government, where he earned enough money to help his family escape to America. He became a barber and owned one of the first gymnasiums in the area. He was a very positive thinker, believing in mind-over-matter. His grandmother passed away while Jim was in Vietnam, and his grandfather never got over it. He always talked about her in the present tense until the day he died.

Jim told me that the morning his grandmother died; Grandpa had made breakfast for her. Jim warned me that to this day, her breakfast was in saran wrap on a shelf inside the refrigerator.

Jim also said that in the bathroom I would find different colors of round cloths. Grandpa would squeeze the water out of his washcloths and leave them around the sink. Jim explained that to undo them, you would have to rewet them. Of course, I thought Jim was exaggerating, until the first thing I noticed in the bathroom were the colorful cloth balls around the sink. I picked up one, realizing that it was as hard as a golf ball. Grandpa's tremendous strength squeezed every drop of water out of it.

Years later at a Qi Gong Seminar in Orlando, the only person I ever witnessed come close to Grandpa's strength was a Chinese Sensei. Our instructor introduced him as eighty-five-years-old as he placed a bucket of mud on a table. We watched the Sensei reach into the bucket, pull out a handful of mud, and shape it into a ball. He then began squeezing the ball of mud until all the water dripped out of his hand. Next, he opened the palm of his hand, blowing dust out into the audience. The power of mind-over-matter is real.

Another one of Jim's stories which made me question if Jim was stretching the truth, involved the circus coming to town. The Ringmaster would have a deep ditch dug. Then, they would drive a car straddling the ditch and offer to pay money if anyone could pick up the car. Grandpa picked up the car, even though he was only five feet tall, which landed him the title of 'Little Strong Man' from the Ringmaster. Grandpa showed me the newspaper article, complete with a picture of him in the ditch holding up the car.

Jim also told me the story that Grandpa would go around the same circus with a $100.00 bill. He offered to give it to the man who could lift his thumb as he held it down. Even the Strong

Man of Circus couldn't lift his thumb. He even let Jim try in front of me, and Grandpa's finger didn't budge. Of course, his incredible, hand strength inspired Jim so much that all the way to CA and PA, he would squeeze a hand gripper. I attribute this to Jim later becoming a Chiropractor. It takes tremendous hand strength to manipulate bones into place. He actually broke three of them during the first year.

Grandpa's Incredible Strength

Little did I know that very soon I would witness Grandpa pick up a car with me inside. It happened the very next morning when Jim started his first day working at the fencing company. Grandpa kept talking about Grandma in the present tense, so much that he had me believing that she was alive. So, I asked him where she was. He got very excited and asked me if I wanted to go and see her. I agreed, even though it was starting to snow. Being from Florida I didn't even own a coat. I was wearing a green and white plaid mini-skirt, thin long-sleeved, white-ruffled blouse, and black, hip boots. So, Spooky (our black cat) and I got into the 1967 Cadillac and left to see Grandma.

As we drove through town and into the countryside the snow began coming down harder. I remember asking Grandpa if we should turn around, but he said that the Cadillac was heavy and good in snow. Several miles outside of town on a long, winding road Grandpa finally turned into the cemetery. It was a large cemetery with huge trees among the monuments, and narrow, winding roads that seemed to go on forever in different directions.

We finally stopped by a large, pine tree, and Grandpa got out. He opened the door for me, and we walked around the tree.

20

He bent down and wiped the snow away from her headstone. Grandpa was very religious, and he asked me if I would pray with him. In his prayer, he introduced me to Grandma as Jimmy's new girlfriend, and he was glad to see their grandson happy again.

As he continued a thick fog settled over the cemetery. Grandpa asked me to sit in the car to wait for him out of the cold. He said he wanted to be alone with Grandma for a moment. It seemed to take quite a long time for him to return. I remember while I was waiting for him, all kind of thoughts came into my head. It was like something out of a horror show watching the thick, eerie fog roll past the car in a cemetery. The wind was blowing the snow sideways making it even harder to see through. I looked out the side mirror and couldn't see the car tracks on the road. Then, I began worrying about getting stuck out there, and no one would know where we were.

When Grandpa finally got back into the car, he had some cash in his hand and placed it in his wallet. I remembered it smelled musty. Then, he started the car and tried to back up. The tires spun around, sliding sideways toward the tree. He tried to pull forward a bit and that didn't work. Then, he asked me if I knew how to drive? I told him I could, but I've never driven in snow.

With God All Things Are Possible

This is when I witnessed Grandpa's incredible strength. Grandpa told me to sit in the driver's seat as he got out. I saw from the rearview mirror, he took a shovel out of the trunk and cleared two tracks behind the car to the road. After putting the shovel away, he told me to put my foot on the brake and wait for further instructions. A few seconds later, I felt the back of the car

21

start to lift and shift to the right. I quickly glanced again and saw that Grandpa was holding up the back of the car and moving it onto the cleared tracks.

He asked me to roll the window down and listen to his instructions. He preceded to guide me until all my tires were on the cleared tracks. He then got back in the driver's seat and backed out to the road. By the Grace of God, we made it out of the cemetery and home.

Being curious as I wrote this, I checked with Siri the stats on a 1967 Cadillac. It weighed 4,676 pounds. Out of all Jim's siblings, I'm honored that God allowed me to witness Grandpa's unusual mind-over-matter and tremendous strength. But isn't that the way Jesus taught His disciples? If you believe, there is nothing impossible with God.

God Prepared Us For A Large Family

On Saturday, Grandpa took us to visit Jim's aunt and uncle in Ohio. They had a very, large family consisting of eight children. It was awesome at the dinner table with the older children helping with the younger ones with their plates. That's when Jim and I knew we wanted a large family. I'd never witnessed anything like it. We could feel the strong bonds of love in the family. That's what we wanted in our family.

However, Pennsylvania and Ohio weren't where God wanted us to call home. Jim's job with the fencing company didn't last more than a week. It was hard on Jim's back, and the daughter kept trying to throw herself at him.

Chapter Four

Listening To The Holy Spirit

It was in March when Jim and I left Pennsylvania and headed back to Florida after morning prayer. By this time, we added Psalms 91 to our morning, prayer routine. Psalms 91 is titled by the Psalmist King David as the 'Assurance of God's Protection.'

Jim said his father, Fred, read this scripture every morning while he was stationed in Hawaii, during the surprise Japanese attack on Pearl Harbor in WWII. He was one of the lucky soldiers who came home from the war because he trusted the promise God made in that scripture. When Jim went to Vietnam, Fred reminded Jim to say it every morning and he would return. Jim and I learned to recite it, and to this day I say it daily.

Realizing the Gift's in the Scriptures

It was snowing off and on as we left PA. We were on I-95 approaching Brea, North Carolina, behind a station wagon with two young kids in the back giving us peace signs. We followed them over a mountain, noticing on the way down, there was a sheet of ice across the entire freeway, including the grassy median. I remember a yellow Corvette Stingray was spinning around in the median like a top. The station wagon slowly made it across the sheet of ice. But as we slowly followed them, the Volkswagen started to slide, spinning around several times before sliding off the side of the mountain, flipping over and over, hitting on all sides.

Jim held onto the steering wheel and stayed inside the van. But I wasn't as lucky. At that time, the Volkswagen seats were bolted to the floor and not the car frame. As a result, still strapped in the seat I flew through the camper as it flipped, being hit with everything inside as the back doors burst open. I flew out of the van still seated, hitting the ground as it continued to tumble down the mountain. The last thing I remembered was heading straight for a large boulder.

I was still unconscious when Jim, along with the adults in the station wagon found me. Again, our travel prayer for safety saved our lives. The only scratch Jim received was when Spooky scratched him when he tried to pick him up. What saved my life was that I was shorter than the seat's headrest. I ended up with cuts and bruises all over my body, and a pounding, migraine headache.

It took a while for the EMT's to arrive. While talking with the ER Doctor via radio, they checked my vitals, placed a cervical collar around my neck, and carefully strapped me onto a flat board. It took a while to get me stable enough to carry me up the mountain to the road. They were to immediately transport me to the Emergency Room. My eyes were dilated, and they didn't know the extent of my concussion and head injuries. The police officer had radioed ahead for a tow truck for the camper. Jim got into the ambulance holding Spooky. They explained that they cannot transport animals in an ambulance.

So, what would two, young people in total shock do? Jim told the ambulance to leave without us as the tow truck arrived. And what would the EMT's legally do? They argued with Jim about my injuries; and then Jim signed a release, and they left us on the side of the road.

They're sat Jim and I hugging each other with Spooky, watching the tow truck drag our VW Camper back up to the side of the road using long cables. The driver wanted to tow the camper to a mechanic near his station, but again we would have to take Spooky with us. Bringing an animal was also against that company's regulations.

Jim asked him if he thought the car was drivable, even though the battery was hanging out of the side of the van. We had just enough money to stay one night in a hotel and for the gas back to his parent's house.

The tow truck driver felt sorry for us and helped Jim fasten a makeshift holder for the battery. That secured it enough, so it wouldn't dangle all the way home. He also had a wooden box in his truck that we used as a seat for me, since my seat was in pieces at the bottom of the mountain.

I was petrified getting back inside the camper. Jim assured me that God protected us by reciting (Psalms 91:11-12) "For He will give his angels charge of you to guard you in all your ways. On their hands they will bear you up, lest you dash your foot against a stone." The large, stone boulder was the last thing I remember heading directly towards. That boulder was my stone, so to say. The angels must have picked me up, because I wasn't in the seat or close to the boulder.

First Stop - Church to Thank God

Jim stopped at the first Catholic Church we found in town for us to thank God for our survival. Since I wasn't baptized and couldn't stand without Jim's help, he explained to the priest what had just happened and asked him to baptize me. The priest refused, since I hadn't taken RCIA Classes to join the church.

25

Now, what would a recently returned soldier from a warzone in Vietnam do? After all he just survived a major car accident with his new girlfriend. Jim got upset, stopped at the Baptismal Font by the front, double doors, baptized me in front of the priest, in the name of The Father, The Son, and The Holy Spirit. The priest watched but didn't say a word against it. We left with the priest following us outside. He watched us from the steps get into our pathetic, broken van with the battery secured outside by the rear tire on a makeshift platform. Then, the priest hurried to the passenger side, saw I was sitting on a wooden box, and said he'd pray that we got home safely to Florida. We thanked him and left.

A few blocks later, we found a hotel for the night. I was weak, stiff, and hurting all over my body that I could hardly move. By this time, the adrenaline was wearing off. As soon as Jim carried me into our room, he examined me from head to toe for cuts, bruises, and possible broken bones. The details of the accident and fact that I was badly injured began to set in my mind. I began to panic and cry, complaining that the top of my head hurt.

Jim tried to calm me down by making a joke about the kitty litter in my long, blonde hair. That only made me feel worse, and I cried harder. That's when he touched the top of my head, and I passed out again. He told me later that he tried to bring me around and couldn't, so he took me to the Emergency Room at the nearby hospital. I woke up in the hospital.

After the doctor examined me, along with x-rays, he said I was one lucky girl to live through the accident with no broken bones, and minimal injuries. He gave me a few scripts for pain medication, something to help me sleep, and released me.

After I fell asleep that night, Jim called his parents and told them what happened. Twila was so upset after Jim told her what happened to me that when she called my mother, they believed I was dead.

The next morning while Jim checked us out of the hotel, I called my mother. I noticed she was crying when she answered the phone. Hearing my voice, she screamed hysterically and dropped the phone. My father picked up the phone and told me that Twila said I died in the accident. They had been up all-night crying. I assured Dad that I was badly injured, but very much alive, and that we were on our way home. Mom did get back on the phone with me, and thanked God I was alive. We talked for a few minutes concerning what happened to me. I told them that we'd see them soon and I loved them.

We drove slowly back to Ormond Beach, Florida, with me sitting on the wooden box. We stayed with Jim's parents for a while. My parents took me to my doctor, and he confirmed I had a concussion causing migraine headaches. It was great being around our immediate family again. However, Jim had bad memories of Ormond concerning his first wife, so we decided to move to Tampa near Jim's older brother and his family. We stayed with them for a few months until we saved enough money to get our first apartment.

The Holy Spirit Saved Me In Tampa

By this time, I was barely pregnant with our first child. Jim secured a job working at the Exchange Bank in downtown Tampa. We found a tiny apartment above a two-story house that two sisters had converted their upstairs into two apartments. We entered through a long, straight stairway on the outside, near the middle of the house. This led up to a long hallway with no windows on either side. On both sides of the hall were two apartments. The front doors were staggered for more privacy. The apartment door on the left was by the stairs. Our apartment's door was on the right near the end of the hallway.

We were so excited to finally have our own place to call home. We called it our Choo-Choo, Train Apartment. We literally could sit up in bed, look through the living room, kitchen, and out the bathroom window. We still didn't have a car, but we were finally on the right track. There was also a small grocery store, and a Catholic Church close enough for us to walk. Everything was going smoothly until one afternoon. Jim always came home for lunch to save money. He had just left to return back to work for the afternoon.

I was sitting across from the front door at the kitchen table, writing a letter to my mother when suddenly, I felt like something evil was standing behind me. I turned to look and there was nothing but the door. But the feeling got worse, and I felt extremely cold. I said a prayer, asking Heavenly Father to protect me. That's when I felt strongly that I must move away from the door. When I hesitated, I heard the words 'move now' inside my head. I quietly slid the chair back and hurried inside our bedroom.

We didn't have cell phones at the time or even a phone inside our apartment. Jim wasn't due home for several hours. The only way I could call Jim was to leave through the front door, walk down the hallway, and go downstairs to use our landlord's phone. That's when I heard the voice again telling me to 'hide in the bedroom.'

At first, I thought I could open the window over our bed, crawl out on the roof, and jump down from there. Except, I was

28

barely pregnant, and it was too far for me to jump. Then, I heard the voice tell me to 'hide in the closet'. I quickly hid behind the hanging clothes. By this time, I now could hear the doorknob moving around. Someone was trying to open our door. I continued quietly praying for God to protect me.

The Holy Spirit Also Warned Jim

At the same time, I was being warned Jim had just gotten back to work, when he suddenly had a strong feeling that I was in grave danger. He never experienced anything like that, so he kept working. But the feeling got so strong that he told his boss. His boss told him to go home and check on me. Jim calmly walked out of the bank and then ran home as fast as he could.

As Jim rushed upstairs and turned into the hallway, he saw our neighbor trying to open our door. He was wearing full, tactical, military gear with a M16 Rifle in his hand. His countenance clearly edgy, causing his hand to shake while struggling to open our door.

In Vietnam Jim worked in psychological warfare, so he calmly and very slowly approached him holding his hands up calling the soldier by name. Trying to diffuse the situation, Jim told the soldier that he used the same rifle in Vietnam. Jim continued calmly talking with him, trying to gravitate the soldier away from our door and get him to put the rifle down.

When the soldier didn't put the rifle down, Jim tried to figure out what triggered the sudden change in his behavior. Jim slowly changed the subject to get him to talk about himself. Maybe, something happened in his family. But he wasn't buying it. He still wasn't making sense, just babbling as he tried to converse. Jim then realized that the soldier was very young, like he was when he deployed to Vietnam.

Jim switched to talking about himself. He told the soldier that he volunteered to go to Vietnam, so his brother wouldn't be deployed. His brother's new wife just found out that their first baby was on the way. When that didn't work either, Jim shifted to talking about the stress of being only eighteen and sent into the middle of an active warzone in a faraway country, halfway across the world. That finally struck a common ground for the soldier to relate to Jim. He calmed down, finally giving Jim eye contact as he clearly spoke.

As they continued talking, the soldier finally lowered his rifle. He admitted that he had just enlisted and was new on the base. Two men threatened him at his job. With God's continued help, Jim was able to talk him into going back to his apartment and call his Commanding Officer to report the incidence. Jim offered to help him and walked with him back to his apartment.

Jim went inside his apartment and stayed with him while he talked with his Commander. Jim overheard the commander order him to immediately return to the base and report straight to his office. He was to speak with no one.

The soldier thanked Jim for helping him. Jim stayed with him making sure he put all his guns away. They continued talking as he left his apartment and locked his door. Jim walked with him downstairs, and out of the building to his car. After he drove away, Jim hurried upstairs to our apartment.

In the closet, I couldn't hear anything that was happening in the hallway. I had no clue that Jim had left work and rushed home. It seemed like forever until I heard our door open. I didn't know who it was, so I kept quiet, not moving a muscle.

Jim finally called my name when he didn't see me inside. With tears of fear and joy streaming down my cheeks, I ran to him. He told me what happened at work and what was happening in the hallway. We immediately said a prayer thanking God that we were safe. We checked from our bedroom window to make sure the soldier's car was still gone, before we went downstairs to talk to our landlords.

The sisters were shocked learning about the ordeal and let us out of the Lease Agreement. One walked us out of their house, while the other sister called the police.

We spent the night at Jim's brother's house for safety. It was hard for both of us to fall asleep. The reality of what just happened finally hit us. If it wasn't for The Holy Spirit warning both of us, and us acting immediately upon His warning, I would have been murdered, and possibly the sister's downstairs. The soldier was clearly traumatized by his co-workers to the point of no return.

There was no reason for the soldier, our neighbor, to be at my door in that frame of mind. I had only been kind to him. The last thing Jim and I talked with him about was that we just found out that I was pregnant. He seemed very happy for us.

The next morning Jim's brother took us to the Dodge dealership near his house. Since Jim worked at the bank for a few months, he received a credit card. We used the card for the down payment on our first car. It was a white, 1969 Dodge Charger with a black, vinal roof, and red, leather interior. Now that we had wheels, we located a Justice of the Peace and got married before leaving town.

We must have been the first couple the female Justice of the Peace married. We still talk about how she was so nervous. She kept bobbing her head from side-to-side and we could hardly understand what she was saying, since she couldn't stop smiling as she performed the ceremony. Her husband was our witness.

We stopped by our apartment to get what little things we owned, including our cat Spooky. The sisters thanked Jim again for diffusing the situation. Immediately after we left them, a police officer arrived and took the report, he told them that likely they would have been his next victims. He said with the seriousness of the intent to commit murder; he was going straight to the Military Base to talk with the Commanding Officer. As a result of both the military and police quick investigation, the Military Police escorted the soldier back to the apartment long enough to pack his things and give the landlord the key. Then, they escorted him off the property in a miliary vehicle and left.

The sisters offered for us to stay in our apartment. We explained that it was very traumatic for both of us. We only came back to pick up our things before heading back to the Daytona area.

God Is Always With You

After the birth of our first child, Jeremy, suddenly our apartment was too small, with the crib, changing table, diaper pail, and dresser added to our tiny, one bedroom triplex. Jim was back at Daytona Beach Community College, and we needed to find something closer to school. We had been together now almost two years and kept up with all our prayers. I should tell you that we still pray together to this day.

We found an older, two-bedroom, garage apartment in Daytona Beach. I remember when we were looking at it, noting the wooden slats in the living room floor were far enough apart that we could see our car parked underneath it in the garage. As

32

for the apartment, it wasn't the Taj Mahal, but it was all we could afford on our budget. Little did I know that in this unsafe neighborhood that God would soon warn me of eminent danger within the first few weeks.

The kitchen was small, consisting of a sink with barely a countertop, if you could call it that. It had a huge stove that took up most of the room. Our dishes were stored under the open part of the pathetic countertop which had two, short shelves. That left no place for our pots and pans, so we kept them on the small kitchen table. Needless to say, when we ate, the extra pots and pans were moved to the floor.

That's when Jim decided to build a wooden shelf above the sink. His Seabreeze High School shop class was paying off. It didn't take him long to install it. That made the cooking and cleanup a lot easier, and less embarrassing when friends or family stopped by.

Another major snag was that it didn't have a shower in the bathroom. I had to wash my long, blonde hair in the kitchen sink.

It was the day after Jim put the shelf over the sink, when I decided to wash my hair after Jim left for class. Jeremy had just gone down for a morning nap, so I had a perfect moment to wash it before he woke up again. I placed my shampoo and conditioner on the floor, and my towel on the kitchen table behind me.

I had just lathered up my hair when I heard a voice in my head say, 'move away from the sink now!' I heard it two more times before I turned off the water, squeezed my soapy hair out, and turned around to reach my towel. I thought maybe I needed to check on the baby. But as soon as I reached for my towel, I heard a loud crash behind me. I turned back and saw that the entire shelf had pulled out of the wall. The wooden shelf and

33

everything on it fell into the sink. Believe me, I said a prayer thanking Heavenly Father immediately!

When Jim got home a few hours later, he was mortified. He remembered that he forgot to use molly bolts to hold the screws in the plasterboard. Without the molly bolts the added weight of the pots and pans caused it to pull away from the wall.

Even though he hung the shelving unit back on the wall with molly bolts, I never trusted it. By this time, Jim had already been accepted into Palmer College of Chiropractic, and we were weeks away from moving. We decided to leave for an early registration. Again, we packed up everything we owned in a U-Haul, said goodbye to our family, and God led us to Davenport, Iowa.

Chapter Five

The Communion of Saints

Daily travel prayer would once again spare our lives on the journey to Palmer College. My Uncle Otis was a Chiropractor and the first doctor to relieve Jim's back pain since Vietnam. It was Otis and later Dr. Walter Aiken who mentored Jim into becoming a Chiropractor. We wanted to stop in Pine Bluff, Arkansas and visit with my Uncle Otis and Aunt Peggy.

After a long, exhausting drive with a baby, we were finally nearing our destination. The excitement of visiting with them on our way to Palmer, would be the perfect beginning to a long, four-years stay in Davenport, Iowa, while Jim was in school.

We had just left the freeway entering a two-lane, country road towards their home which was just outside the city limits of Pine Bluff. A couple of miles down the road was a sign for a sharp curve ahead. The vegetation on both sides of the road had been cleared, so there was no obstruction to our view. The traffic was light that day, only a few cars had passed us going into town. As we approached the curve, we came up behind a semi-truck carrying long-metal irrigation pipes held together by several large chains wrapped around them. There was no way around the truck before the curve since the double-yellow line had just begun. As the truck entered the curve, Jim noticed the truck bed was extended to carry the extra-long cargo. He mentioned he had seen those kinds of trucks carrying bombs in Vietnam.

Without any warning right before our eyes, the back chain broke triggering the pipes to loosen, causing them at first to shake and wobble around. Jim glanced at the deep ditches on both sides of the road, then checked his rearview mirror, before stepping on the brakes, trying to put distance between us. But as our car slowed down, the second and third chains snapped due to the movement and shift of weight. The back of the truck bed began swaying from side-to-side off the road, clearly the driver was losing control.

Since the driver couldn't stop along with the speed, the pipes began flying off the truck across both sides of the road, bouncing twice as high as they were long. The pipes headed straight for our car. Jim had no choice but to maneuver around and through them. With the deep ditches on either side of the road, there was no place else to go. I started calling out the Name of Jesus constantly for His protection, watching the pipes hitting the pavement, and bouncing around our car and trailer like the child's game of pick-up sticks. We could hear the loud sounds of the metal pipes pinging as they hit the pavement.

It all happened so fast it was surreal, almost like shifting into slow motion as we maneuvered through them. The driver of the truck was still desperately trying to regain control. Some pipes hit so hard they dinted the pavement. They continued hitting all around the car and U-Haul until the very last two, which when freed from the ones above them, went airborne. One flew over our car and the last one was heading parallel to our windshield. That's when Jim hit the brakes swerving way off the road into a deep ditch, which broke the front axile.

When the car finally halted, Jim and I turned to check on the baby. Jeremy was strapped into his car seat and didn't budge. He was screaming by this time, so I reached in the diaper bag by my feet and handed him a bottle. At this time, my body was shaking so badly; I couldn't stand up to get out of the car and bring him up front with us.

What seemed like an hour only took about five minutes of Jim maneuvering through the flying objects. Our voices were shaky as we began talking about what had just happened. Jim said we were seconds from the impact of the pipe smashing through our windshield, killing us.

He said through it all, he could hear me calling the Name of Jesus. It was by the Grace of God; the last pipe suddenly lifted over the roof barely missing us at the last second.

I reminded Jim that when you call upon the Most Powerful Name in the Universe, it gets the attention of God, and He comes to your aide. Jesus surely came to our aide! We couldn't stop praising Jesus for this wonderful miracle.

After we regained our composure, Jim saw the driver had finally stopped way ahead of us. He was safe and already slowly walking towards our car. The terrified driver leaned on the door, holding himself up by the open window, and fell to his knees. His voice also was shaky as he managed to tell us that he used his CB-Radio to call the police, and they were on the way.

When he saw Jeremy in the backseat, he held back tears thanking God that none of us were injured; much less killed. I can't remember his exact words, but it was that the Lord was looking after all of us today. He confessed that he could barely stop the rig. It was the hardest thing he had ever done in his life.

When the police, and ambulances arrived looking at the scene, they expected fatalities. They were amazed that none of us were injured. They said the road would be closed for hours cleaning up the objects. The EMT's checked us out. They assured me that Jeremy was fine. One of the police officers called Uncle Otis and waited with us until Otis picked us up. An officer at the roadblock had to let Otis on the scene. Otis was shocked when he saw the devastation.

We stayed at his house while the car was repaired, and he paid for it. Since I was still in terrible pain with migraine headaches from our first accident, he also took x-rays and adjusted me, Jim, and Jeremy. We all needed it after that ordeal.

It was great visiting with him and Peggy. We were all looking forward to meeting each other at Chiropractic Seminars around the country after Jim graduated. Otis was glad that Jim would see Grandpa Hiers more often that he was able to and check his spine. He explained that all the years of farming left Grandpa Hiers with terrible, back pain. He was stubborn and refused to go to a Chiropractor in Moultrie. Otis really missed his family in Georgia, but his heart was in Arkansas.

God's Plan for Our Destiny Changed

A few days later, we continued our way to Palmer as soon as the car was ready. Little did we know, that would be the last time we saw Uncle Otis alive. All our dreams of meeting him and Peggy at seminars never came to fruition. After Jim graduated in June, he accepted an associate position in Ohio.

This position was also a blessing from God. Just before Jim was about to graduate, we realized that we had absolutely no money to move, and nowhere to go. Jim's father had told us that he couldn't afford to help us anymore. Here we were with two small children and one on the way. We both got on our knees several times praying to God for the answer.

A week before graduation, Dr. Evan Beane came to Palmer looking for an associate to work with him in Defiance, Ohio. He met with most of the graduating doctors and chose Jim over all of them. That was the answer to our prayers. He even paid for our travel to Ohio from Iowa.

38

In October our third child was overdue. My parents had arrived to help me with the arrival of the new baby, Melody, and Jeremy. The next morning, I gave birth to Keely. Of course, I came home very early the next morning. I never stayed in the hospital very long after the birth of my children.

Mom was nervous about taking care of a baby less than twenty-four hours old. She couldn't get over how small Keely was. My father was in 'hog-heaven' playing with Jeremy and Melody. He called Melody his 'movie star'. He took a picture of her wearing a long, red dress, and her favorite white sunglasses. On her arm, she always carried her purse over her bent elbow, so it dangled as she walked. He said she reminded him of me at that age.

It was a great time until the next morning, Mom received a phone call from her older, brother Roy. Uncle Otis had suddenly died of a heart attack. Mom was crying as she packed their bags, not wanting to leave me after barely given birth. Jim and I assured her that we would be fine, and Aunt Peggy, and the kids needed her more. They left our house within the hour on the way to Pine Bluff.

It's hard for us to understand what God has planned for our destiny. He moves people in and out of our paths to guide us at His pleasure. Philippians 2:13 "For God is at work in you, both to will and to work, for His good pleasure."

Growing up I only saw Uncle Otis a few times in my life since they lived in Arkansas. It was always a treat for the entire Hiers Family to get together for a family reunion at Grandpa Hiers' house in Moultrie. Only once, my father took us on a vacation to visit them. Yet even though I wasn't as close to Otis as my other uncles, God used him to reveal Jim's destiny into becoming a Chiropractor. But it wouldn't be the last time Uncle Otis adjusted Jim in this world.

The Communion of Saints

Jim's practice in Ohio grew quickly, and before we knew it, Jim was seeing quite a few patients a day. Since Chiropractic is a very physical profession, performing side-posture adjustments on the lower backs of heavier adults, including helping them off the table was hard on his own body. Being the Junior Associate he was off on Thursdays and had to work on Saturday. That meant balancing his work and two days off with being a husband, and father to a growing family along with his outside chores.

After Jim had been in practice for a while, Jim came home from work one afternoon with a backache. I noticed he was being very careful not to pick up the kids. When I asked him if he was alright, he told me that he worked on a hefty patient, and afterwards his back began to stiffen. He had Evan adjust him before he came home. After the adjustment, he felt a small improvement, but it was still nagging him. He took a hot shower and went to bed.

In the wee hours of the morning Jim woke up with an unbearable, low, back spasm. His low back injury from Vietnam had come back with a vengeance. He was in such pain; he could barely get out of bed. Since we went to Palmer, we didn't have any pain medications in the house.

But as Catholic's, we believe in the Communion of Saints. That means that if we have faith, we can ask saints, angels, or family member's that have gone before us to help us. Since Otis was the first person to relieve Jim's Vietnam back injury, he asked God for a heavenly intervention. Jim slowly got out of bed, knelt beside it, and prayed that God would allow Otis to adjust him once again.

I woke up to Jim sobbing thanking God for allowing Otis' Spirit to adjust him. When I asked him what happened, Jim said that after he prayed, it felt like Otis pulled something that felt like a string out of his back. The pain immediately stopped. God has an abundance of compassion and miracles waiting for those who call upon Him. Jeremiah 1:12 "Then the Lord said to me, 'You have seen well for I am watching over My Word to perform it.'" God truly listens to the prayers within our hearts.

Chapter Six

God Places People in Our Path

It wasn't long after that miracle when Jim's Senior Partner changed the contract. Instead of renting a small office which they split all the cost, now he wanted to build a new clinic with Jim still paying half of the bills. At that time, we were making fantastic money and saving $2,000.00 a week. We bought our first house at the Country Club. The new office contract meant we would be buried in debt on a building that Jim wouldn't own a part of. So, with prayer we sold our house quickly, and off we went back to Port Orange, Florida.

Jim bought a map of the area, and circled where he wanted to open a clinic, and where our new home would be. With the sale of our house and patient's records, we had enough money for a down payment on a new house, and a build out of the new clinic. Our clinic happened to be across the street from my parent's house on Ridgewood Ave.

Three major things happened in 1981 to our family. First a single friend at church, Renee, was in an automobile accident. She needed back surgery causing her to stay in the hospital lying flat for six weeks. She had two small children with no one to take care of them. It was during the recession that Pres. Jimmy Carter brought upon the United States. With the high inflation of his 'so-called' economic policies, food prices skyrocketed, and gas shortages were nationwide.

Renee's children went to the Elementary School across the Port Orange Bridge, about six miles from where my children attended. Our pastor asked us if we could take care of them, since we had children their ages. When Jim and I discussed it, he

42

began listing all the problems we would encounter. Secondly, I was barely pregnant again and caring for two more small children with the five we already had, would mean more work for me.

Jim also worried that our house was already too small for our expanding family. Where would they sleep? The extra financial stresses of food and gas shortages meant long lines at the pump. Jim noted that both schools started and got out at the same time. How could I physically have everyone ready and fed in the morning and be at both places at the same time? Remember, Proverbs 6:2 with my Father's Blessing? "You are snared in the utterance of your lips, caught in the words of your mouth."

I boldly told Jim that we are helping a single mother in distress. We can bring her children's beds to our house and double up in the children's room. God will fill the gas tank in the van and grant us the extra funds; that's the least of our problems. I'll explain to the principal at their school about Renee's situation and the time problem. I'll simply drop our children off first and take her children.

We believe in the Almighty God of Heaven and Earth, of things visible and invisible. When I called the school, the principal instantly agreed to help me. As for Proverbs 6:2, we were truly blessed by my words of faith. Your words can bless you or curse you.

Jim's practice also seemed to double immediately; that cleared our money issue. I never ran out of gas, and every time I pulled into a station, the lines were short. The principal had cancer and was blessed too. He never showed signs of not feeling well, always greeting us with a smile. He always waited out front for me to drop them off in the morning and waited with them after school until I could pick them up.

God Healed Jeremy

The third major thing that happened was after Renee could finally care for her children. Danielle was about six months old when Jeremy was diagnosed with Eosinophilic Granuloma of the C4 Vertebra.

Jeremy was a little accident prone at that time. He ended up with several minor, seemingly, innocent injuries to his neck. Jim x-rayed him after each injury when he continued complaining that his neck hurt. The third and final injury happened when his cousin, Robbie built a wooden fort in my parent's backyard. Jeremy climbed up the ladder and the trap door accidently fell on the top of his head. Jeremy was back in the office getting x-rayed. That's when Jim noticed that the C4 cervical, vertebral bone was starting to disappear.

We took Jeremy to Dr. Gillespie, an Orthopedic Surgeon, for a second opinion. While Jeremy laid on the exam table behind me, Dr. Gillespie said, "I don't know what's wrong with your son, but he's going to die."

Those words struck a major nerve within me, and I loudly declared to Dr. Gillespie, "My son will live and not die! God will help us find the right doctor and find a cure!" Psalms 118:17 "I shall not die, but I shall live and recount the deeds of the Lords." Then, I stormed out of his office with my son!

And that's exactly what happened. Matthew 15:11 "It's not what goes into your mouth that defiles you; you are defiled by the words that come out of your mouth." Jesus taught his disciples that your words are powerful. Jesus called his disciples not for who they were, but who they could become. An example was Simon Peter who had a hot temper, swore, and carried a sword. Yet, he became the Rock of the Catholic Church and the First Pope.

We went home and immediately called our pastor for a blessing. After the blessing, he told us to take Jeremy to Shand's Teaching Hospital in Gainesville. With Danielle still nursing, I had to leave her and the other children with my parents to travel with Jeremy. We had a van with a bench seat in the back where Jeremy had to lay down during the four-hour trip, wearing a neck brace to keep his neck straight.

As soon as we arrived, a team of doctors met us outside the front door carefully helping Jeremy on a gurney and taking him straight to be examined. After x-rays, blood work, and an MRI they concluded that he had Eosinophilic Granuloma at the C4 Vertebra. They scheduled him for surgery in two days. Jim decided to stay with Jeremy, while I went home to be with the other children.

That night, seeing Jeremy's empty bed, I laid across it crying uncontrollably for God to please save our son. I must admit, that was the first time in my life I felt defeated. My faith was being tested, and I felt like Job. All kind of scenarios from the enemy began filling my head. With Jim at the hospital miles away, I called a neighbor who came over and comforted me. He stayed and talked with me until I was back in control of my emotions and faith. Like Job, I had to trust in the Lord, not just during the good times, but in times like this.

Seek God and He Will Answer

But God never left me or Jeremy. Jeremiah 17:7 "But blessed to the man who trusts in the Lord, whose confidence is in Him." I returned to Shand's the morning before Jeremy underwent surgery with a renewed hope. From inside the operating room after several hours, the surgeon called us in the waiting room, to report that the disease was treatable. He explained that Jim had caught it in time, and that the disease was common in the long bones. Usually, the non-malignant tumor would begin to decay for a few weeks and then re-calcify. But since Jeremy's was in the cervical region, he would have to undergo a few radiation treatments and be put on steroids for a while.

Jim had to return to work. I stayed three more days with Jeremy while he was undergoing treatment. I began praying for all the patients sitting next to me with worse illnesses. I've learned to stay in faith understanding the importance of the scriptures. Jeremiah 30:17 "For I will restore health to you, and your wounds I will heal," says the Lord.

We decided it was time for new surroundings, and we wanted the children to see more of God's world. So, we moved to the mountains of Utah. Once again, our parents were heartbroken that we took away their grandchildren.

Chapter Seven

Of All Things Visible And Invisible

So, we moved to Bountiful, Utah. The terrain was extremely different than Florida. We loved to hike with the kids in the mountains during the summer and play in the snow in the winter. By this time, Jeremy's cervical spine had healed, and Jim put the older kids in karate. We had two boys a year apart also during this time.

Jeremy became quite the young entrepreneur starting a neighbor Karate Dojo in our basement for about a year. His first belt review was on a Friday evening with the parents present. Jim and I were so proud. Saturday morning, it was our job to take Jeremy to buy the belts for his students. This meant we had to drive into Salt Lake City to the Dojo Jim and our children attended to purchase the belts. I remember it was freezing, but no new snow in the forecast.

Jim put the other seven children in the car while I finished dressing our newborn, Zachary.

Heed God's Warning Signs

As I started to leave my bedroom, suddenly I couldn't go past the doorway into the hallway. It was like an invisible barrier was stopping me. I could hear Jim blowing the horn for me to hurry, but I couldn't move. Then, I felt cold, and death all around me. I just stood there, holding Zachary in fear. I could hear Jim getting impatient honking the horn longer and longer for me to hurry, but I couldn't move a muscle. It was as if The Holy Spirit or my Guardian Angel held me back, and the feeling of cold and death heightened. I was horrified.

Finally, I heard Jim entering the house through the garage door, walking to the steps, and storming up each step. I watched him reach the top step, turn towards me, glaring at me as he walked down the long hallway. Before he reached me his anger kindled as I clutched Zachary closer to my heart inside the doorway.

He immediately asked me what was wrong. I told Jim that the Holy Spirit or my Guardian Angel wouldn't let me leave this room. I feel cold, and death all around me. He put his arms around me, and said, "Then, let's ask God to protect us." We knelt beside our bed and prayed that our family would be safe in our travels today.

As soon as we got into the car, we prayed again with the family. We had an hour drive into Salt Lake City on I-15, which was six lanes across at that time. About halfway there, Jim and I were discussing that the freeway was extremely busy, even for a Saturday morning.

We were in one of the two, middle lanes with cars all around us traveling about 75 mph up a steep hill. As we started down the hill still following several cars without warning, like dominoes falling, one by one each car in our lane quickly changed into different lanes like a practiced dance routine. When the last vehicle directly in front of us darted to the left, we were heading straight into a disabled truck. The driver was standing behind his broken truck warning people to change lanes. The back axle of his truck had broken, and one of the back tires was sideways.

It all happened so fast. We saw the look in his eyes as he threw his hands across his face knowing the worse. Jim slammed on the brakes along with the cars behind us, forcing our van to skid into the far, right lane to miss him. Jim and I were in awe as the lanes actually seemed to widen, giving our van enough space to change lanes at the same time as the car right beside us. All traffic behind us came to a screeching halt.

Miraculous Warning

We were truly saved by a miraculous warning from our Lord. With our van at that speed, hitting the driver, and his truck would have killed all of us. The Holy Spirit or my Guardian Angel not only warned me with a resolute feeling of cold and death all around me but wouldn't let me leave my bedroom. Then, after we said two prayers for safety in our travels, the lanes in the road widen for not only our passage, but the car next to us as well. Looking back today, the Lord saved quite a few people that day. As our van would have exploded, the cars traveling around us could have wrecked or caught fire.

Jim and I praised God for warning me and keeping us safe all the way to pick up the karate belts and back home. To this day, I often wonder what happened to the driver of the truck, and what went through his mind that miraculous day.

God Speaks to Our Hearts

Also in 1984, Jim and I had another experience with God protecting Zachary and Tyler. They were both very young at the time. Tyler was fifteen months old, and Zachary was six months old when we experienced our first Canyon Winds at about 100 mph. It was late and we were getting ready for bed when the winds suddenly picked up out of nowhere. Jim glanced out the bathroom window noticing parts of our six-foot wooden fence had blown over. He asked me to help him grab some of our outside furniture off the patio.

I had just finished nursing Zachary, so we put him in his crib in the nursery next to our room. Tyler was sleeping in his youth bed under the window. Leaving the nursery, we heard a gust of wind shaking the nursery window. We both got a bad feeling in the pit of our stomachs and turned, noticing the glass in the window moving. We'd never seen anything like it.

I immediately ran back and picked up Zachary as Jim grabbed Tyler. As we left the room the window broke, scattering glass all over the room. Jim shut the door quickly to keep it from hitting us in the hallway. When we returned to the room, most of the glass had landed in the crib, and some in the youth bed. Both boys would have been badly cut. It was a miracle that Jim and I both had the same feeling to turn around at the same time. No other window on that side of the house broke.

A Cry From Heaven

A few days later, after putting the younger children to bed and waiting for Jim to check on the older ones, our family witnessed a loud cry from heaven. Melody, and Keely had just finished their homework and turned off their light. Jim came upstairs after checking on Jeremy in the basement and making sure the doors were locked. We got ready for bed and had just lied down talking about our day. We heard, what sounded like it came from high above the hallway a loud and distinct cry of a newborn baby.

I sat up and told Jim, "that's not one of the boys." Jim and I were getting up to check on the children, when Keely hurried to our bedroom doorway. "Mom," she said, "I heard a loud baby cry

50

coming from somewhere in the hallway. I checked on Tyler and Zachary in the nursery, and they are sound asleep. Mom, it didn't sound like them either."

I told her that we also heard a baby cry, and didn't recognize the voice. We waited with Keely for a few minutes and never heard it again. But to this very day, we all remember it as if it were yesterday. But my favorite saying is 'Coincidence is God's way of staying anonymous.' Less than a month later, I found out I was pregnant with baby number nine. Seven months later, our daughter, Shandelle was born in January of 1986 the day before Jeremy's birthday. It appeared that the Lord shared a supernatural announcement that Shandy was on the way.

Chapter Eight

Angels Are Around Us

We decided to move back to the East Coast to Marietta close to the Atlanta area. The weather there had the changes of seasons that we liked, and Jim had connections at Life Chiropractic College. Jim sold the practice, and at the same time he had a job waiting for him at the college. It took awhile for us to sell our home, so we were forced to rent.

Jim's younger brother, Charlie lived with his stepsister, Penny in Marietta where they had two young children with a third on the way. It was odd that their children only had one set of grandparents, my stepmother and my father-in-law. It was nice finally having a friendship with a sister-in-law and our children got to know their cousins. Penny and I would get together each week for the children to play. Their children were the same ages as my youngest children.

One thing I noticed off the bat, was that they fought a lot! That only made me more determined to help them, since it was evident that they needed God in their lives. So, I added them to my Rosary Petitions when I said my daily Rosary. Jim and I started having them over on the weekends for dinner.

Who would have thought that our friendships would only last for a short length of time. The last time they came over, we were having an enjoyable evening until it started getting late, and snowing. Charlie decided to go home before the roads got bad. The Atlanta Area doesn't have the snow removal program, since it barely snows there.

I was getting the coats out of the closet by the front door. Penny stepped away a bit helping Jared put on his jacket. Charlie was trying to put on Leah's jacket. I can't remember what started the argument. Penny was holding their three-year-old son Jared, about four feet away from Charlie when he said something that upset her. She got very aggravated and threw Jared towards Charlie. In shock, I caught Jared in midair. Charlie wouldn't have been able to catch him while holding Leah. That upset Penny even more, she headed back to the kitchen screaming that she was going to call the police.

Jim followed her and Charlie into the kitchen with Charlie pleading with her to stop. I'd never seen anything like it, and I didn't want the police to come to our house with my children downstairs asleep. Unbeknown to us, Penny had a reason for the commotion involving the police. And she planned to do it at my house.

Angels Are God's Messengers

It was about midnight, and I yelled, "Heavenly Father, we need help!" At that very instant the doorbell behind me rang. I turned around in shock and opened the door. There stood a beautiful, young woman with waist-length, dark-blonde hair, which was parted down the middle. She wore a coat made of two-to-three-foot long, white feathers that seemed to hug close to her body. She looked straight at me, and then sternly glared over my left shoulder toward the fireplace by the kitchen entrance. Then, her eyes shifted back to me and said, "I was told you needed help." I was in shock and said, "No, we don't!" and slammed the door in her face.

I didn't know my eleven-year-old daughter, Keely, was hiding in the coat closet by the door. Melody and Jeremy ran up from the top of the basement steps, where they also had a perfect view of her standing at the door. Keely widened the closet door, and said, "Mom, she was barefooted, and her feet weren't touching the ground! She was an angel!"

Keely immediately opened the front door, and the angel was gone. Jim and Charlie heard the commotion and ran to the door. There were no footprints in the snow on the small porch to the door, no footprints on the steps down to the sidewalk, nor the sidewalk to the street. Jim, Charlie, Keely, Melody, Jeremy, and I ran outside. I noticed Penny stayed inside. We looked everywhere, even up on the roof. There was no sign an angel or that anyone was there at all.

When we got back into the house, Penny had calmed down and wanted to immediately leave. However, the kids and I were busy explaining to Jim and Charlie what transpired. We all shared the exact same story, except for Keely and I saw the angel with a different color of hair. Penny made it clear that she didn't want to hear our story, and she was getting agitated, so Charlie had to take them home.

The next day Jim and I didn't hear from either of them. I called a few times to check on Penny and ask her if she saw the angel, but she didn't answer. I figured she was busy with the children, since they were up late the night before. It wasn't until Charlie got home from work late that afternoon, when he called Jim telling us that Penny and the children were gone. Charlie had called his father to see if he knew anything. Fred admitted that he and Pat had picked them up that morning. It had already been planned. That was the reason for her sudden argument and demanding to call the police. She wanted a police report on Charlie to further her cause to leave him.

Penny sued Charlie for desertion, even though she is the person that deserted him. She made a false allegation against Charlie and won custody of the three children. Charlie never saw his children again. I never got the chance to talk with Penny about the angel at our door that night or saw her again. But that's not quite the ending of this story. . .

28 Years Later

God's timing isn't always our timing. Twenty-eight years later, Jim and I were living in Port Orange, Florida. By this time, all of our children had grown up and left home. Charlie was living in Utah when he got a phone call from his ex-wife, Penny. Penny lived on the Georgia/Alabama border. She had gotten his number from their parents. Charlie hadn't seen or heard from her or his children during that time.

Now their son, Jared, was going through a terrible divorce and his wife was using the same false allegation against him. The Florida Courts had jurisdiction over the divorce and custody battle of the three children. Penny needed Charlie to meet her and Jared in Florida to help him get custody.

Charlie checked the internet and found out that the court was less than an hour from our house. So, he asked us if they could stay at our house in Port Orange to save the cost of two hotel rooms.

At first, we wanted nothing to do with either of them. I talked with Jim's twin sisters, and they didn't want to get involved with that mess either. But Charlie was insistent, and we finally said yes. Charlie arrived the day before Penny and Jared.

The next evening proved to be a bitter-sweet reunion. I did invite Penny's oldest brother, Danny and his wife Kathy over for support. Danny is Jim and Charlie's stepbrother, and we've always had a great relationship with him and his wife.

Shortly after dinner, Danny and Kathy left, since it was a work night. It was still early, so we decided to go for a swim. Jared went to bed since they had to be in Melbourne at 8:00 am the next morning. While we were in the pool, Charlie and Penny were getting along very well. I remember Penny said, "If I knew you were going to be this much fun, I would have stayed married to you." By this time, it was getting late and chilly, so that was my cue to go inside to change clothes and get ready for bed.

A few minutes later, Jim opened the sliding glass door from the pool to our bedroom. "Kathe, you need to hear what Penny started to tell us. Hurry and come out here!"

As soon as I sat at the table on the lanai, Penny asked me if I remembered the angel at my door in Georgia. I told her that I've told everyone over the years about the beautiful angel that talked to me. And I couldn't believe I slammed the door in her face. I've apologized to her, and God ever since then.

Penny continued, "I was standing in the Great Room by the fireplace just outside the kitchen. The angel looked over your left shoulder at me." I told her that I remembered the angel looking over my shoulder in that direction. Jim had told her that I saw a beautiful angel. Penny told me that she didn't see a beautiful angel. She saw an ugly angel with long, black hair and long, black feathers like a coat close to her body. She didn't run outside that night with us, because she thought it was the Angel of Death coming for her. She was afraid that if she went outside, the angel would have killed her. I retold her about my encounter with the angel.

Then I asked her, "If you thought it was the Angel of Death, why did you go through with your plans to leave Charlie?"

She didn't say a word, got out of the pool, picked up her towel off the chair, and went inside to her room. They left early the next morning with Jared. That's when I learned that even when God intervenes, we have our free agency, and He steps back.

Chapter Nine

I Will Never Leave You Or Forsake You

During that twenty-eight-year period before finally talking with Penny about the angel, Jim opened a practice in Marietta. One of the patients Jim would encounter would lead us to the Monastery of The Holy Spirit in Conyers, GA.

This patient, Kathy H. would lead us to St. Catherine of Sienna Catholic Church in Kennesaw. The first day we attended, Kathy met us in the parking lot with her family and sat with us. That was the beginning of a great friendship. Kathy was a nurse, and visited the Monastery in Conyers, Georgia several times a month to check on Fr. M. J. Joachim Tierney, one of the Monk Priest.

Fr. Tierney suffered from chronic, low, back pain. So, Kathy arranged on a Saturday morning for Jim to meet Fr. Tierney to see if he could help him and offered to pay for his treatment. Since it was an hour away, we decided to take the family. Little did we know that it would be a meeting that our family would never forget, and the beginning of a close friendship with Fr. Tierney.

He was a Marion Priest devoted to the Blessed Mother Mary. He began treatments at our clinic the next week. Since the Monastery was so far away, and Fr. Tierney needed to come in three times a week to get his problem out of the acute stage, the Abbot approved him to spend a week at our house.

It was awesome having Mass every morning in our home. Father Tierney brought everything he needed to say Mass and give us sacrament. At young ages, Fr. Tierney taught Tyler and Zachary to be his Altar Servers. Fr. Tierney was so inspiring, I learned so much about our faith from him. He also said daily Rosary with me, which strengthened my consecration to the Blessed Mother.

Jesus Appears To Me

When I was weakened in distress over the loss of my last child, Jesus came to me with His overflowing love.

I was three months pregnant with our eleventh child, who was due in November. I was still helping Jim in the new clinic. A man came into the office without an appointment, but we had time before lunch to see him. He presented with no signs of trauma, so Jim asked me to help him with the x-rays. My job was to position the patient in different positions for a full set. Something I had done many times.

Jim took the man's measurements and left the room to set the machine. But as I positioned the patient for the first x-ray, without warning, he fainted. Instinctively, I caught him before he hit the floor. I felt something pull in my abdomen but didn't think anything of it. I finished working that day feeling just fine. We went home and I fixed dinner. After dinner, I helped Jim get the younger children ready for bed as usual. I was fine when Jim and I went to bed.

Jim and Jeremy had plans for a hike the next morning, so we went to bed early. I woke up a few times during the middle of the night to use the restroom with no problems. However, about 5:00 am I woke up to use the restroom and felt like I was having a few labor pains. Long story short, I ended up having a miscarriage to the point that I almost hemorrhaged to death.

Jim told me afterwards, that I was in congestive heart failure when the ambulance driver took the exit off the freeway at 90 mph. I lost so much blood, complicated with the rare Blood Type AB-, it was touch and go for a while.

My recovery took several weeks for me to regain my strength. I was devasted. We named the child, Payton James Hether. To this day, I have a Christmas decoration hanging on our ceiling fan above our bed of a little, brown bear wearing a white, turtleneck sweater. Where the heart would be is cut out with a heart-shaped, emerald birthstone. Payton was due in November around Melody's birthday. Each year, Jim and I take the bear down and place it on our 12' Christmas Tree under the Angel on the top of the tree. After Christmas, we put it back over our bed.

After I physically recovered, but was still mourning the loss of Payton, I was taking a hot shower one morning. The bathroom was filled with steam as a flashback of that dreadful morning when I realized, I was miscarrying filled my mind. I remembered that morning getting into a hot shower trying to stop my labor, but instead my body began losing the baby. I remembered thinking that women seeking abortions asked for this to happen to them and was even more horrified.

As my mind continued rehearsing that morning, I began panicking and fled the shower, putting my towel around me. Even though the room was filled with steam, I glanced at the mirror over the bathroom vanity. The left side of the mirror began across from the shower.

I clearly saw the entire, right side of a man's head in the mirror. As I stared at it, the steam continued to clear only in that spot until an entire man's head emerged. He had light- brown, shoulder-length hair, parted down the middle with no bangs. I'll never forget starring into His light-blue eyes, which I seemed to fall into and felt safe. Without using words, He told me that everything was going to be alright. Instantly, I felt the warmth of

His gentle, peace, and grace encompass me. That's when as mysterious as He appeared, He disappeared.

I quickly got dressed and called Jim to tell him what happened. Next, I called Fr. Tierney and told him. He told me that everything would be alright and made an appointment to have lunch with me in a few days, before his appointment with Jim at the clinic.

Jesus Came To Me

A few days later, I prepared lunch for Fr. Tierney to join us. When he arrived, he had the monthly Catholic Magazine folded under his arm along with a wrapped gift for me. I began retelling him about the man I saw in the mirror. At that time, I had never seen a picture of the Sacred Heart of Jesus. I wasn't raised Catholic, and there was a brief time we had been away from the church.

When Fr. Tierney showed me the cover of the magazine, I began to cry. It was the Man I saw in the mirror. The same face, light-brown hair, and light-blue eyes! The same eyes I seemed to fall into, that told me everything was going to be alright!

Fr. Tierney, then asked me to open the gift. It was a framed painting of the Sacred Heart of Jesus. Fr. Tierney said he knew it was Jesus the moment I said, "I fell into His eyes and felt the warmth of His gentle, peace, and grace encompass me." Fr. Tierney confided that other people over the years have had similar experiences. He was so sure he brought the painting to give to me. Later, I found out that Kathy H. had recently given the painting to him. That painting hangs by my front door above a picture of the Sacred Heart of Mary from that moment to this day. They are a constant reminder of the love Mary and Jesus have for all of God's children.

Apparitions of Mother Mary

At the beginning of the next month on the first Saturday, Fr. Tierney invited us to attend the Apparition of Mother Mary near the Monastery. Little did I know that it would be the beginning of several years of attending the Apparitions to hear Mother Mary's messages.

The Apparitions were at the farmhouse of Nancy Fowler and her family. We would park in an onion field, but the air was filled with the scent of roses, a sign of Mother Mary's presence as she descended into the house. Children in the large crowd would see Mother Mary descend from heaven and start pointing to the sky, telling what they saw. On a PA System with speakers set up outside, Nancy would tell the people Mother Mary's messages or warnings.

One day on July 13, 1993, we bought a Polaroid Camera to take the pictures of Mary ascending from the house back to the heavens. I brought the camera but forgot to bring the film. A lady sitting next to us gave us some film. Children stood up after Nancy said Mary was leaving and started pointing at the sky and crying, "we see angels around the house."

Chase was sixteen years old at the time, and said, "Mom, give me the camera. I see the angels and Mother Mary." Jim handed him the camera and Chase took several pictures as quick as he could. The first picture (see figure #1 in the back of the book) shows the ring of angels around the roof of the house. The second picture shows Mary ascending from the roof (see figure #2) and the last one shows the Host, the round wafer which the priest changes into the Body of Jesus during the Transubstantiation of the Eucharist. Mary is clearly shown standing through the Eucharist. In the picture you can see her head above the Host, her body through it, and her dress and feet under it (see figure #3). Mother Mary always said, "Come to me, and I will show you, my Son."

The pictures Chase took were so profound that we stopped by the Monastery on the way home to show Fr. Tierney. We waited for him in the garden by three life-sized, white marble statues. It was about 2:00 pm and a bright, sunny day. I took a picture of a white, marble statue of Mother Mary (see figure #4, page 192) and then turned around and took a picture of Jesus. (see figure #5 page 193). These pictures were also profound. At the time, something was deeply disturbing me, and I was praying for peace of mind. Only the Lord and I knew what it was about. I did ask Fr. Tierney to pray for me but did not say why.

Jesus Suffering On The Cross

When Fr. Tierney joined us, I showed him the pictures. With the statue of Mary, I said, "Fr. Tierney, who is this a statue of?" He looked at it, smiled, and said, "Oh deary, I know that statue well. It is a statue of Mary, but you captured a picture of Jesus." (see figure #4 page 192) Instead of Mary, the shadows on the face show Jesus' face, long hair, and beard. Then, I showed Fr. Tierney the picture of the white, marble statue of Jesus. Fr. Tierney said, "Oh deary, Jesus answered your prayer. (see picture #5 page 193) You captured Jesus' suffering on the cross. He is telling you that life isn't perfect, even He had to suffer on the cross. Give up your problem to Him and go on with your life."

In the picture there is a smaller, white, marble statue that someone placed at the foot of Jesus. But the statue of Jesus looks like Him at Golgotha hanging on the Cross. You can see the sweat on His flesh-toned arms, abdomen, and legs. Jesus was giving me a sign to stand steadfast in faith with Him. To this day, the pictures look the exact same way they did, the day I took them!

Sometimes I look at these old pictures taken by a Polaroid camera (35 yrs. ago) with old technology which normally would fade with time. But the ones I took are as perfect as the day I took them. I can still hear the words of Fr. Tierney when I was going through one of the worse valleys of my life and showed them to him. "Oh deary, I know that statue well. Instead of Mary, you captured a picture of Jesus." And the white, marble statue of Jesus that turned lifelike. "Oh deary, Jesus answered your prayer. You captured Jesus' suffering on the Cross." Now years later, as I read the scriptures in Bible Study, I realize those pictures are miraculously saved as a witness to Christ our Savior.

Luke 12:48 states, "From everyone who has been given much, much will be demanded, and from the one who has been entrusted with much, much more will be asked."

I have learned one thing as did the Twelve Disciples who walked with Jesus, and St. Paul called by Jesus on the road to Damascus, all the prophets, Nancy Fowler seeing the Apparitions of Mary, myself, and many others who have come forth with similar circumstances. It's not easy to withstand the critics, but it's something "you can never deny."

Years later at age thirty-one, Charlie Kirk of Turning Point USA knew this very principle and lived by it. He started his company at age eighteen in his garage. His mission was to bring Jesus back to the youth of the world. He visited College Campuses worldwide teaching the students the importance of putting God, families, and country, back into their lives. He was assassinated in Provo, Utah on September 10, 2025, by a group of horrible, godless young men. But Charlie did not die in vain. As a result of this heinous crime, people around the world have noticed a 'shift' back to Our Lord and Savior. The internet is filled with thousands of stories of people who no longer believed in Christ that have joined churches, bought Bibles, and are bringing their families back to the Lord.

Chapter Ten

A Statue Of Mary Turns To Flesh

I continued saying my daily Rosary as Jeremy began Life Chiropractic College. It was after the Rodney King incident in Atlanta that caused rioting for months in the city. Earlier that day, Fr. Tierney told me about Archangel St. Raphael, who is God's physician, and over the safety of families, peace, joy, health, and travel. Fr. Tierney said that sometimes St. Raphael shows up as a big dog to help people as he did in the scriptures with Tobias and his father.

All though, in the scriptures St. Raphael unexpectantly appeared to Tobias and his father and stated his name was Azarias, and he would travel with the young Tobias. But I believe in Fr. Tierney's version, and this is the reason why. Mark 11:22-24 (The key to this scripture is believing.) And Jesus answered them, "Have faith in God. Truly, I say to you, whoever says to this mountain, 'Be taken up and cast into the sea,' it will be done for him. Therefore, I tell you, whatever you ask in prayer, believe that you receive it, and you will."

St. Raphael Appears

Jeremy came home from college and told us that he was going with friends to a bar in downtown Atlanta, which I strongly opposed him going, because of the racial tension. But Jeremy explained that he would be with several friends from college. He said there was a designated driver, and they would be fine. Jim agreed that he should go with his friends. As a single father, it was important for him to fraternize with other students in college. I immediately prayed that St. Raphael would watch over Jeremy in his travels.

Jim and I were in bed when Jeremy called needing a ride home. He told Jim that he was in an alley between two buildings near the bar where rioters kept passing by. A big, ugly, mangy, brown dog entered the alley and sat down beside him. Whenever anyone neared the alley, he would growl loudly, and they hurried past. He said he called us from the phonebooth in front of the alley when it was safe. The dog followed him, sitting down in front of the door to block it, growling when anyone passed them. Jim told him to stay there, and he would hurry to get him. This is before GPS. Jim had no idea where the address was and started looking for a map on his desk.

Luckily, Keely and her boyfriend came home as Jim was about to leave. We told them the story and they knew exactly where the street was. They had gone to a concert near there a few days earlier. They went with Jim to bring Jeremy home. When they saw Jeremy in the phone booth, they pulled over for him to get inside the van. The first thing Jeremy said to them was, "Did you see the size of that dog? He stayed by the door of the phonebooth until you got here and then let me out!"

Neither Jim, Keely, nor her boyfriend saw any dog. When they got home and told me about it, I told them about St. Raphael and thanked him for saving Jeremy. Later, you'll read how I honor St. Raphael in two books that I have recently written.

A Stalled Van
Another time, Jim and I were taking the children school shopping at a mall in Kennesaw, GA. Our van was the first to stop

at the red light at a major intersection. The light changed to green for us to go but the van suddenly stalled, which it had never done before. Jim struggled to restart the van as a dump truck loaded with rocks sped through the red light on the opposite side of the intersection. We instantly thanked Heavenly Father for answering our family travel prayer. We could have been injured or killed.

Mother Mary Appeared To Me

It was shortly after that, when I met and became friends with a new parishioner at our church, Sandy. She was diagnosed with Multiple Sclerosis and was having a hard time walking and driving. After telling her about the Apparitions and Fr. Tierney, she began attending them with me.

Fr. Tierney told us about a Healing Mass at a Catholic Church in Buckhead near Roswell, thirty minutes from my house. Sandy and I decided to go. I brought my daughter, Danielle, while Jim stayed home with the other children. As we entered the building, there was a long hallway to the entrance of the sanctuary. Halfway down was a catwalk which branched off to a life-sized statue of Mother Mary holding Baby Jesus.

I had never been to a Healing Mass and didn't know what to expect, so we hurried into the sanctuary and found seats. Sandy explained that after Mass, the priest would ask people to form a line in front of the altar. Several men would stand behind them to catch people as the priest would say a short prayer while touching their heads with a relic which caused them to fall straight back. Of course, I was a skeptic and said, "I'll never fall."

When it came time for our pew to line up, Danielle was on my left and Sandy on my right. The priest started from the right side of the line. In my peripheral vision, I saw Sandy fall backwards. The next thing I knew the priest touched my forehead, I blacked out, and a man was helping me up. Danielle was being helped up at the same time. It was something that I never experienced before. Even though I didn't remember falling, somehow, I felt like something shifted in my consciousness. A few minutes later, I understood why I had the feeling. Although, I must be honest, I never expected a miraculous visitation would happen to me as I left the church.

The Statue of Mary Turned To Flesh

As we were leaving the Sanctuary, something seemed to call me to the statue of the Blessed Mother holding Baby Jesus. We walked down the catwalk to the statue. As I gazed at the statue, praying for the specific miracle I needed, Mary turned to flesh. I saw Mother Mary smile at me. I heard Sandy behind me begin to cry, falling to her knees. She too witnessed the statue turning to flesh. My daughter, Danielle, knelt to the right of me and kept trying to reach out and touch the hem of Mother Mary's dress. But each time, before she touched it, she would withdraw her hand.

I could hear other people leaving the sanctuary passing in the hallway stopping and falling to their knees in astonishment saying, "look at the statue!" The statue of Mother Mary has come to life! Who is the lady praying in front of Mary!" I turned around to see them kneeling in the hallway. When I turned back, the statue was back to its original shape.

As we left the catwalk, each of us smelled strongly of roses, a sign of Mary's presence. The people in the hallway were the first to notice the strong scent of roses on me. When they

69

asked me what I was praying for, I told them that I was working on a project to help Mother Mary stop abortion. I asked Mother Mary to help me get the project to someone who could help me bring it to fruition.

Why Mother Mary Appeared

The reason I was drawn to the Statue of Mary that night began years earlier. I had attended so many Apparitions, listening to Mother Mary each time say the latest numbers of aborted babies in America. She also said that she cried tears of blood for them. She warned that if America didn't stop abortion and repent, there would be a great punishment. A well-deserved punishment was dealt to America in 2016. At the time Mary warned us that day, I didn't think America could stoop any lower. How could I have known years later that the American government would be taken over in 2016 from within by a coup with an evil agenda?

In 2019 Governor Ralph Northam of Virgina, a 'Red Democratic State' passed a law that abortions can be done up until birth and even after birth. It reads that the Mother and doctor can decide to either keep or terminate the baby's life. That is called infanticide which is pure and simple murder. I watched the news the day the law passed in Virginia, and the lawmakers were dancing with joy in the courtroom. It was like watching demons filled with excitement partying. I was sick to my stomach and knelt immediately down apologizing to God that those people could be so devilish. The Catholic Church along with other churches and organizations are fighting to stop this in the Supreme Court.

Honestly, Mary's words that day in Conyers pierced my heart like a dagger thrust deep into my, very soul. America passed a sinful law so grievous, that the Mother of Jesus cried tears of blood for each child torn from the womb. My thoughts went to Luke 22:44 which details how Jesus, during His prayer in the Garden of Gethsemane, was in such agony that His sweat became like drops of blood falling to the ground.

As a mother, I couldn't fathom the enormity of Her grief, since we are all her children through Christ our Lord. When Jesus was on the Cross, He said in John 19:26-27. "When Jesus saw His mother there, and the disciple whom He loved standing nearby, He said to Her, 'Woman, here is your son,' and to the disciple, 'Here is your mother.' From that time on, John took Mary into his home." It represented Jesus telling us that Mary is the mother of all God's children.

Abortion had become an ordinary word by this time in America. I kept praying the Rosary for Mother Mary to help me find a way to help her stop this crime against God and mankind. That's when Mother Mary inspired me to write a manuscript for a book, movie, and soundtrack. Together, that media would quickly spread Her message not only to America but throughout the world. God doesn't make mistakes, and every child is formed in His likeness. Jeremiah 1:5 "Before I formed you in the womb I knew you, and before you were born, I consecrated you; I appointed you a prophet to the nations."

I had just finished the manuscript, along with the lyrics of seven songs that would fit within the movie for a soundtrack. The real band that touched my heart was coming to Atlanta, and I needed to get a copy of the manuscript, also containing the lyrics for a movie soundtrack for them to review.

Since Fr. Tierney inspired me to attend the Apparitions, I told him about my idea. For the main character, I would use my first name and his last name for the heroine. He gave me a blessing that I would write something spectacular to help Our Lady. As I continued to pray, I felt very strongly that I needed to target the youth.

The younger generations were used to hearing the word abortion like it was something legal that women did. To show the different side of the spectrum, I felt very strongly the need to expose why society was failing within the storyline. Rock Music was very popular, and my teens were glued to a TV Show called MTV. One of the most famous groups at the time was Def Leppard. I used different names for my characters and changed the name of the band. The characters in the manuscript have nothing to do with the actual people of that band nor their beliefs. I just needed a focal point to aide in the realism of my characters. The storyline was about two people accidently meeting and falling deeply in love. Except for one major problem, their professions collided. One was on the cover of every magazine, and one had to stay in the shadows.

When we got home about 1:00 am, Jim met us at the front door frightened that it took so long. Cell phones were in the developing stages, not like today, so he had no clue where we were. The first thing Jim said to me was, "Where were you?" He then stepped back and said, "You smell so strongly of roses." Danielle went to bed while I sat down and told him what happened that night.

The next day, since it was just before Christmas, I wrapped the manuscript like a Christmas present with a big, bright, colorful bow. Jim and I drove to the Atlanta Convention Center where Def Leppard was performing. We easily found the area that led backstage without anyone stopping us. At that very moment, a stagehand was coming back from the concession stand. Without hesitation I asked him if he would give it to Def Leppard. He agreed and took the package backstage for me. It was unbelievably easy. Surely, the Blessed Mother helped us every step of the way. Jim and I were so excited on the way home.

The very next day, one of our patients called me with an extra ticket for the final night, including backstage passes to meet the band members asking me if I wanted to go. I was so excited that I would be able to meet them while they had my manuscript. Except the one thing I didn't count on was Jim refused to let me go!

Again, it was so evident that Mother Mary had arranged the meeting. I had no idea the patient had tickets to the concert. It was no coincidence that one of her friends at the last minute got sick, so she called me. She had gotten my phone number from where she worked at the cable company. Even with me explaining to Jim that Mother Mary was helping me like last night to meet the very people who could help us, Jim refused to listen.

About a month later, on Christmas morning a package was delivered to me. It was the manuscript wrapped in the same, special wrapping paper and bow that I used. Some band members read it, along with the song lyrics I copyrighted for the movie. One of the members must have been eating something, while running his fingers through the lyrics, because there were greasy smudges. Several months later, the band came out with two new songs that fit perfectly for a movie soundtrack. There was a note inside the manuscript that read, "We don't get involved in politics." I believe that is why Mother Mary arranged for me to meet the band. With Her help, I would have pitched the manuscript for both novel, movie, and soundtrack. I have no doubt that the outcome would have been different.

Even though Mother Mary helped me get the manuscript to Def Leppard, without the right pitch from me, they had their free agency not to get involved. I had to respect their decision. But that didn't stop me from continuing with a series of books speaking out against other injustices to mankind. It only strengthened my determination.

Years later, Project Chameleon—later known as Project XP38, Project Wraith, and Project Canaveral—continued to reference Mother Mary's message, which remains relevant to contemporary societal issues. Now, we are dealing with human trafficking, child sex crimes, and drugs flowing easily throughout America, and the world.

Abortion was just the beginning of the 'Culture of Death' which Satan had planned to bring down America, and then the world. With the 2024 Election, the spiral has slowed but hasn't stopped the crimes against God and humanity. The good news is that we now have President Donald J. Trump back in the White House, fighting to save the Judeo/Christian values and justice.

Throughout history Mother Mary has appeared trying to turn the world back to Her Son, Jesus of Nazareth. I too will never give up. Once in the presence of Jesus, you never want to turn away from Him.

Other Mother Mary Sightings

Fast forward to August 20, 2024, Jim and I were watching a video on YouTube of the fifteen sightings of Mother Mary's Statues either turning to flesh, blinking Her eyes, or moving. Some people caught sightings on their cell phone cameras. At the time I saw the Statue of Our Lady turn to flesh, along with others. I did tell Fr. Tierney, but it was never documented, so there are sixteen sightings.

Next, we watched a video on St. Juan Diego's Tilma, and the Lady of Guadalupe. Mother Mary is a powerful intercessor. I went to bed feeling that Mother Mary is not finished with me yet. What miracle She begins in us, She will see come to fruition. My then setback, will someday become a setup to help Mary, and Her Son, Our Lord and Savior Jesus Christ.

Chapter Eleven

A 'Shadrack, Meshack, And Abednego Miracle'

When you pray with a contrite heart, God always listens to you, even though those you are praying for don't listen to 'that still small voice.' The scripture in John 9:31 is important because it warns about believing and listening to God. "We know that God does not listen to sinners, but if anyone is a worshiper of God and does His Will, God listens to him."

Just before Jeremy graduated Life Chiropractic College, his car broke down. He was almost over the finish line towards his goal to work with his father. All the years of studying and scrimping to get by was almost over. Then, his car broke down. The repairs would cost more to fix it, than the car was worth. He only needed a used car to drive for a few more months. His goal for all the hard work was to buy a new car.

Since there was a used car dealership near the college, he bought one from there. After driving it for less than a week, it showed signs of having major, electrical problem. By the Grace of God, it was still under a thirty-day guarantee. Luckily, the owner loaned him a courtesy car to use while they repaired his car. The repairs ended up taking almost two months.

Every Friday Jeremy would call to check on the status of the car. Since it was taking so long, Jeremy asked the owner if he would switch the car for another one on the lot. He explained how he needed a dependable car, using it to work several different odd jobs late at night, which required him to take his two, small children with him. Then, during the morning and afternoon bringing and picking them up from my house. He asked the owner if he could even switch to the loaner he was driving now since they were about the same price. But the owner assured Jeremy that he would have it working perfectly. Almost two months went by before Jeremy got the call that his car was done. He had just picked up the children from my house and drove to exchange cars.

I doubted the car's repairs would hold, given its electrical issues and the time it was kept. From past experiences of friends growing up, used car dealerships always bought the cheapest cars at an auction to resell. Basically, they cleaned them up and sold them with the words 'as is' in the contract. I warned Jeremy when he left my house to be careful driving it home, and if anything seemed 'funny' for him to turn around and take it back. I said a travel prayer before he left.

It was noontime, when Jeremy left the dealership and was just entering I-75 with the children in their car seats in the backseat. As he was entering the on-ramp a voice came over the radio saying, "Your car is on fire," two times. He checked the radio, and it wasn't turned on. He heard it a third time just as clear as the first two times. He glanced in his rearview mirror and saw that smoke and flames were billowing out the back of his car. He immediately pulled over before entering the freeway.

The driver behind him called her ex-husband, the Fire Chief reporting the car fire as she pulled over to help him. Jeremy got out of the car and was standing in flames as he opened the back door. He didn't have time to take the children out of their car seats, so he unbuckled the car seats. He quickly tossed each child, still in the seats, for the lady to catch them. It happened that a Fire Truck was on the freeway close to the scene. When the Fire Truck arrived, they were away from the flames taking the children out of their car seats.

A local Fox News station's crew arrived and filmed the incident for the 6:00 pm nightly news. Jeremy and the lady were interviewed explaining what transpired. The newscaster reported that it was a miracle that neither Jeremy's clothes, nor his shoes were burned. Neither was his skin or the hair on his arms and legs. He didn't even smell of smoke.

Jim and I call it our Shadrack, Meshack, Abednego, Jeremy, Jonathan, and Heather Miracle. The news called it unexplainable, but we know the voice on the radio was either Jeremy's guardian angel or The Lord answering my prayer.

Jim Brings a Woman Back to Life

It wasn't long after this miracle that God would use Jim to perform a miracle for another family. The State of Georgia passed a law cancelling Chiropractic from car insurance plans. This was a devasting blow to all Chiropractors. Our bills stayed the same and our income began slowly dwindling as the months went by. It got so bad, that one night Jim came to bed with a shredded, one-dollar bill inside a sandwich baggy, he told me with tears in his eyes, that it was our last dollar.

For some reason, this triggered Jim to remember the actor, Danny Thomas' story before he became famous. Mr. Thomas was an entertainer trying to get started in the industry. He was down to his last dollar one day standing in front a Catholic Church in Detroit. He went inside and put his last dollar in the poor box in front of the statue of St. Jude Thaddeus. His prayer was that St. Jude would help him find his way in life. That prayer was the turning point in his career that made him famous.

As a thank you to St. Jude, Mr. Thomas started the St. Jude's Children Research Hospital for children with ALSAC

(American Lebanese Syrian Associated Charites). This charity funds pediatric cancer research. When Jim finished the story, we both prayed for God's help with our finances. I remember it was hard falling asleep that night.

About 3:00 am, I awoke to Jim getting dressed for work. He said that after praying, he fell asleep and woke up about an hour ago. He felt strongly that God wanted him to go to the clinic and start going over the past due billing. Maye he could find enough missed accounts that slipped through billing to pull us out of this current crisis. After all, the office was extremely busy. So, he left telling me that somehow it would be alright, and that God always pulled us through tough times. I finally fell back asleep praying for God to help Jim. But that's not quite the kind of help God had in mind.

About an hour later, Jim called me with adrenaline still pumping throughout his veins. His voice was filled with excitement as he shared a miraculous story.

It began as soon as Jim arrived at the clinic and was getting out of the car. He heard the tires of a speeding car screeching to a halt at the other end of the strip-mall. The door flung open as a woman fell to the pavement screaming for help while grabbing her chest. Jim rushed to help her. The store attendant walked out of the door to see what was happening. Jim yelled for him to call 911 as the woman died in his arms. Jim immediately started CPR and was able to bring her back to life by the time the ambulance and police arrived.

The EMT's quickly took over for Jim until she was stable enough to transport. Jim and the attendant answered questions from the police as the EMT's transported her to the nearest hospital. That was another blessing of God, since the hospital was only a mile away.

Three days later, a man in his forties with grown children and small grandchildren came into our office. I was working the front desk. They were all crying as they stopped to talk with me. The father with tears streaming down his cheeks asked me if he could speak to Dr. Hether. He said that he and his family wanted to meet the doctor that brought his wife back to life a few days ago in this parking lot. She had just passed away, and they had just left the hospital. Even though the waiting room was packed, I took them back to Jim's private office. I located Jim and sent him to talk to them.

On the way home, Jim explained that God had sent him to the office early that morning not for us, but to help that family. The woman had just passed away and they came straight to our office. Jim was able to bring her back long enough to say goodbye to her family. She had never shown any signs of heart problems, and it was a total shock to the family. One of her daughters had harsh words a week earlier and they had time to make it right. God works in mysterious ways. The daughter would have never forgiven herself.

God did bless us after that happened. We were able to sell our practice and move back to Port Orange a few months later.

The Miraculous Transformation of Dennis Jones

It wasn't long after we opened our new clinic on Nova Road, when God would introduce another person for a specific reason into our lives. We were blessed to watch the transformation of Dennis Jones back to our Lord and Savior. His witness of how Jesus saved him is one of power, love, and self-control. 2 Timothy 1:7 "For God did not give us a spirit of timidity, but a spirit of power, and love, and self-control."

The power and love of Jesus Christ is so powerful now in Dennis' life. In his conversion, he turned from a modern-day version of Saul on the road to Damascus, to dying in sin, forgiven by Jesus, and became like 'an Apostle Paul.' Now every breath in his body lives to bring others to Christ.

Every Friday night, Dennis goes to the Boardwalk in Daytona Beach; to the very place filled with runaways, prostitutes, drug addicts, and alcoholics. He wears a backpack filled with Bibles to give away as he preaches the Good News. Dennis along with a small group of friends have saved over 4,000 souls to date.

Years later after we left Daytona, as I was working on this chapter, Dennis Jones' name flooded my mind. Over the years, we've called on Dennis to pray and help us with one of our adult sons. He was always eager to help and wanted no money in return. God wanted Dennis to share his amazing testimony to help others. After a phone call to Dennis, this is his story in his own words.

I was raised in a Christian home with wonderful, God-fearing parents. But I had a spirit of rebellion. At age twelve, I had a preacher jump on me and threaten to beat me up. That was my excuse to never go back. Then at age thirty-eight, I found myself acting like a teenager, married with five children. I slipped into alcohol and drug addiction. Cocaine became my god.

One afternoon in November of 1993, my heart stopped from a cocaine overdose. I couldn't snort it up my nose any longer. So, I put some cocaine in a shot glass mixed with water and drank it. It felt so good, that I did it again. When I did, I laid back in a waterbed and started tripping. My chest suddenly felt so heavy, it felt like my heart was being pushed out of my body about three feet under the waterbed. About that time, a power and force I can't explain, catapulted me out of the waterbed physically. I landed on my feet. I had no control over my body. It felt like my foot was falling asleep, but it was my whole body.

I had accepted Jesus Christ as my Lord and Savior when I was ten years old and was baptized. I believe the Holy Spirit resided in my heart all my life. All the years of my rebelliousness, lies, hatred, and anger while listening to the devil, The Holy Spirit never left my side. He was patient and never forced me to turn away from sin. He still loves us when we are dead in our sins, and trespasses.

Next, I was carried out of the house. I didn't see angels or the Holy Spirit. I went past my wife, Tamara. I told her that I was having a heart attack and to take me to the hospital. On the way to the hospital, I blacked out (died) in the car.

When I woke up, I was running in a hospital parking lot. I was still under the effects of cocaine, which made everything appear like a cartoon. (Later, I was told that when the doctor put the paddles to me to restart my heart, I jumped up and ran out of the hospital). When the orderlies caught up with me and put me in a wheelchair to take me back to the Emergency Room, I blacked out (died) again.

This time, when I woke up, I was in the most beautiful place I have ever seen. My grandmother was looking at me, sitting on a hill that looked like it was made out of rose petals. I was thinking, "there is no way I can be in heaven." But now, I believe God granted me this grace to prove that heaven is real. His grace and mercy showed me, to be absent from the body is to be present with the Lord. This scripture is in 2 Corinthians 5:8

"We are confident, yes, well pleased rather to be absent from the body and to be present with the Lord."

I never knew of God's love and mercy. I had always lived in fear of dying and death. I was always mad at God asking Him why He made us, just to kill us. Now, I realize that way of thinking was filled with more lies from the devil. Now I know without a shadow of doubt, that Jesus willingly gave up His life for each of us. His death and resurrected paid the price for our salvation to return to the Father.

After this awakening of my soul, I was back into the Emergency Room. I descended back into my body, feet first, from head to toe. This time, I was strapped down with giant, leather straps listening to my heart start and stop. I heard Tamara crying, begging me not to die and leave her with the kids as she watched and listened in fear to what was happening. I couldn't talk because of the amount of cocaine still inside me. I was going crazy listening to the loud sounds of the heart monitor. I constantly heard my heart beat, then flatline, beat again, and flatline.

God showed me through this experience that He has the absolute power over life and death. The scriptures teach that not one hair falls from your head unless He allows it. It was the longest night of my life, not knowing whether I was going to stay with Tamara and the kids or die. Even after being allowed to glimpse into heaven, I had no assurance that I was going there. It had been so long since I prayed. I got Psalms 23 and the Lord's Prayer mixed up, but I was trying to pray for God's help.

Two weeks later, I was still so afraid of dying that I wouldn't take a deep breath. I looked like a scared rabbit in a cage. I was invited to attend a Charismatic, Pentecostal Church. They had the most beautiful worship teams I had ever heard. The

83

music was the hook that God used to draw me closer to Him that Sunday morning. I surrendered to God, asking Him to go ahead and kill me. I don't know how to take my own life. I can't take anymore chaos, turmoil, and fear constantly going through my mind. It was after I surrendered myself to God's Will, that I was able to take a deep breath again.

Sunday night, I attended the service again wanting a change. At the end of the service was an Altar Call, where the pastor asked if anybody needed a miracle to come forward. I went up to the altar with several people. I didn't know what to expect. The pastor laid his hands on the woman next to me and she fell backwards. Someone was standing behind her and caught her. When he put his hands on my head, it felt like fire hit the top of my head, and I felt like I was going to float out through the roof. Then, I started uncontrollably crying and shaking. I was born again in the Spirit.

In the Bible, Acts, Chapter 2, it talks about the Baptism by Fire on the Pentecost. When God sent the Holy Spirit to Peter and the Disciples giving them the power of tongues to teach the Good News to the ends of the earth.

Since that moment, I can take deep breaths again. The chaos, turmoil, and fear in my life are gone. I haven't had the need or want of a drink of alcohol or drugs. To believe in God is easy. To trust in God is to know Him. The only way you know God is to read and learn the scriptures, which is the Word of God. From that moment forward, I live to serve the God of Abraham, Issac, and Jacob.

Chapter Twelve

I Ascended Into God's Realm

As for me with all the moves and everything that transpired throughout the years, I was still working on the book Project Chameleon, which later the title changed to Project: XP38 that the Blessed Mother inspired me to write during the apparitions in Conyers, GA.

I must take a moment to explain the title of my first novel. Project Chameleon was the title of the original print. Jim had a hard time marketing the book. While I was at work one day, he went to Orlando for a meeting with Xulon Press, Publishing Company. After we talked about it, Jim signed with the company, paid them $5,000.00 to represent us.

What we didn't know even though we had already had the copyright and published it with our own Raintree Press Publishing Company, they illegally changed the copyright over to them. Next, we noticed that when we went to the Website and clicked on Project Chameleon, instead of bringing up my book, it led readers to similar books. When we realized that we never received a royalty check, Jim further researched the company and there were many authors documenting the same results.

Then, we noticed that every year Xulon Press would change the spelling of the company's name. Point of interest, not having the money to sue them, I had to re-release the book as Project XP38 under my original copyright. The same thing happened to a Filmmaker friend of ours, Stephen Brown who I'll talk about later.

All through life, I've learned that bad things happen to good people. And, that God always has a plan to get us to our destiny.

Sometimes God's Setbacks Are Setups

It was during the first Easter Vigil after we moved back to Florida that God revealed His plans for me. By then, two boys were on the regular Altar Server schedule. Ironically, it was Tyler and Zachary, who at a young age, first served as Altar Servers when Fr. Tierney stayed at our home in Georgia. They were honored to serve at the Easter Vigil with the Bishop of Orlando, his entourage, several area priests, and other Altar Servers from nearby churches. We went to church very early to reserve our seats towards the front so we could watch the boys.

However, everyone was thinking the same thing, and we ended up sitting in the back of the church in the small chapel. I was devastated; we couldn't see the altar from those seats. All we could do was listen, since the chapel had speakers in the ceiling.

During the Preparations of the Gifts (Eucharist), a miraculous experience occurred. I was kneeling in between Jim and Britt, still upset that I was unable to see the boys on the Altar. Suddenly, it felt as though I left my body, rising way above the room. The ceiling seemed to disappear, since I was looking down on the Altar. Instantly, I sensed that I was in the presence of Deity. Everything happening on the altar seemed magnified with a deeper, spiritual meaning.

After studying the scriptures, I realized I had ascended into God's realm with Him. Together we watched the Bishop performing the Transubstantiation of the bread and wine into the Body and Blood of Jesus.

At that moment, Jesus communicated to me spiritually that I would do something significant and grand on this altar. Without the use of words, I asked Him what could a woman do on a Catholic Altar that would be significant? Jesus understood my question was from the heart. After all, women do not have major rolls on the altar. He lovingly repeated that I would do something major on His Altar, while we observed the clergy beginning to distribute the Eucharist to the parishioners. Jesus repeated the assignment that He had chosen me for a third time and then I felt myself descending back into my body.

Jim nudged me and asked, "Where were you?" I whispered, "I will explain what happened on the way home." Then our pew stood up to take the Eucharist. As I approached the Priest, I felt humbled, and honored to have had the privilege of watching the Bishop perform the Transubstantiation while standing in the very presence of Jesus. As I partook of the Eucharist, it resonated with me that Jesus had chosen me to do something very special for Him on His Altar. Kneeling in the pew, thanking Him for the honor to stand in His presence, I wondered what the Lord of Hosts had in store for me. John 10:14 came to my mind: Jesus said, "I am the Good Shepherd; I know My sheep, and they know Me." My birthday is October 14 which is 10:14.

After the Easter Celebration with refreshments in the Parish Center, on the way home I told Jim and the children what happened. That event marked the beginning of significant changes in my life for His purposes.

God's Plan For Me Begins

During Mass two weeks later, Father Raymond O'Leary announced the need for volunteers to fill various church ministries. He emphasized the importance of contributing our time and talents to further the Kingdom of God. Ushers distributed forms listing the ministries along with pencils, giving us five minutes to provide our information, and select a ministry before collecting the forms.

Our family sat in the front right row, directly in front of the choir. An usher handed the lists to our pew. I reviewed the ministries but saw nothing that fit my interests or schedule. So, I checked 'other' and for some strange reason, I offered to write and direct Biblical Productions for Christmas and Easter.

Jim leaned over showing me that he offered to serve in the Ministry of the Sick and asked me which one I chose. So, I showed him mine.

He immediately asked me why I offered to do productions. I told him that suddenly I felt strongly compelled to do it. Then, he quickly told me to choose something else. But as he said it, an usher appeared picking up our lists.

And here is another mysterious thing that happened, while I was waiting to put mine in the basket, another usher from the left side of the pew held out his basket only for mine. He then quickly turned and went straight to the back of the church towards the Sacristy.

Jim was beside himself and hurried to catch the usher to retrieve my paper, but several people got in his way which slowed him down. The usher with my list walked into the Sacristy and the door closed and locked. So, by the time Jim got to the Sacristy, he couldn't get inside.

On the way home, we both questioned the bizarre episode of events that had just taken place. Then, we simply chalked it up as 'crazy' and agreed nothing would ever come of it.

God's Plan Was Put Into Action

But something major did come of it. A few weeks passed, and we both forgot about it. Jim took the class for the Ministry of the Sick and had already begun going to one of the nursing homes closest to our church. He enjoyed bringing sacrament to the Catholic residents after Sunday Mass. Some of them had no visitors, since their relatives lived up north. Within a few short weeks he felt the joy of serving others.

Another couple of weeks went by, and then Father O'Leary had his assistant call me into his office. We discussed that I had done a few small-scaled shows in our church in Utah, and how bringing the scriptures to life had quite an impact on the parishioners.

I had no idea that Fr. O'Leary was a fan of the theater, nor that he already had someone chosen to help me. As we talked, someone knocked on the door and entered. He introduced me to Mary and explained that he appointed her to help me oversee the production. Then he added with his Australian accent, "If it's going to be on the Altar of Christ, I want it to be first class. Just don't burn me church down." As we left his office, we laughed that the priest just gave a blonde and a redhead an open check book on a first-time musical production.

I spent the rest of spring and summer rewriting and enhancing the Christmas script that I wrote for the church in Utah. I found it unbelievably easy for me. It was as if I had done this my whole life. I created the timeline, listing all the characters, and stage hands needed for a much larger-scale congregation.

The first week in October, I spoke at all four church services asking for parishioners to fill the needed positions. I explained what we were doing and that we would need seamstresses, singers, actors, dancers, musicians, lighting, sound, props, stage managers, and stage hands. For the actors, we needed people from ages newborn to 100 years old.

After Mass, Mary and I had set up a table in the Parish Center where parishioners gathered for coffee, donuts, and fellowship. We signed up several hundred people that weekend.

It was such a success that we did the same thing the next weekend and got over 100 more. I realized one thing that day. God already knew the plethora of talent sitting in our pews when He called me to do the productions.

I had no formal theater education and wasn't a fan of books or theatre. My main qualifications were an active imagination and love for Christ. While checking the signup list, I noticed one parishioner had previously owned Sunco Productions. That was the stage lighting company at Peabody Auditorium in Daytona Beach.

He designed the lighting set, figured out how many microphones we needed, and ran the motherboard for our lighting. Maggie Green signed up for the props position. She too had no formal education in theater, but her granddaughter was attending college up north for Theater Set Design. Maggie went through the script with her and gave me a list of props we needed. John H. signed up to be my Assistant Director. He performed in two of the theatre groups in the Daytona and New Smyrna areas. Leanne signed up to be the Liturgical Dance

Instructor. Several men signed up to be carpenters. And the lists went on. . .

When the Lord told me that I was going to do something significant and big on His Altar, I had no idea that it would take the entire altar and last for several years.

Chapter Thirteen

God's Plan On His Altar

The first year's production was simplified but still a huge success. But as the years went on, the productions got bigger and better.

I also had no idea that Fr. O'Leary invited the Choir Director Dan to add music and singing to the shows. The first two years, Dan read the script and picked the songs to fit the storyline. After that, Dan bought the rights to use different cantatas to perform. My job was to listen to the cantata for that year and write a storyline for the characters to perform around the music. To my surprise, Jesus had that covered and it easily came to me.

The next year, Dan ordered a twenty-foot, tall Living Christmas Tree for the choir members to stand inside. When I was told this surprise, I hurried to church to get a visual of how big of a change this tree would have on the scenes, and movement of the characters.

Staring at the entire altar area, an idea popped into my head. I found Fr. Ray and brought him into the church to explain my dilemma and idea. The baptismal fount was even with the auditorium floor by the steps up to the altar. The carpenters could cover the baptismal fount including the steps with a wooden floor to give us a larger size stage left. I explained that the original choir area would turn into stage right, and the living Christmas Tree would have to be in center stage, due to its height.

At that moment, Fr. Ray reminded me that it was a church, not a theater. He asked me where the altar and the chairs for he and the Deacon would be placed. I looked up towards heaven and spoke. The carpenters would need to build another stage extender in front of the tree with steps up to it. The Altar and the chairs would be placed there.

I'll never forget watching him as he thought for a very long couple of minutes. Then he said, that's a lot of trouble for the tree. I immediately answered him, "Dan surprised me with the tree, too. With its height, that's the only place the tree will fit." He reluctantly agreed, and I thanked him.

We had another issue - the tree was made in China. When assembling it, some of the heavier choir members didn't fit inside. The carpenters had to quickly rebuild it.

The third problem we encountered was at the first dress rehearsal. The hot, stage light shining on some of the choir members caused one to pass out. Praise God, the person next to her caught her before she got hurt. And another person felt the same way and got down from the tree.

When Dan bought the tree, he didn't consider how hot the stage lighting would be for people standing still for 90 minutes. Those with conditions like diabetes or high blood pressure struggled with the heat. This issue hadn't arisen before because actors were usually moving around under the lights, and the choir was not in the line of the heat, since it was over to one side.

A few of the choir members were medical doctors. They suggested we put large fans blowing up from the bottom underneath. Several of our parishioners were EMT's. They offered to stand behind the tree if there was a problem. The Good Lord had that issue covered as well.

God Brought Our Parish Together

By late October, John and I cast the actors and began rehearsals. As the only experienced actors, we taught everyone movement and speech. Mary and her team of seamstresses measured people for costumes. Initially, we rented costumes, but over time, it became more cost-effective to make them.

The year Mary and I decided to make our own costumes left us with some funny memories. While we were in a fabric store selecting various materials for multiple outfits, an unexpected situation arose. During the process of fabric cutting, Mary had to leave abruptly to pick up a child she was babysitting. Consequently, I had to remain in the store as insurance to pay for the cut materials in case Mary did not return.

Another funny story is that Jim and I took one of the artists, Terri who was retired to look for boxes to be used as props. She picked out a large refrigerator box as well as some medium boxes. Luckily, Jim drove his Ford Bronco 4x4. We barely got the boxes inside after lowering the back seats. When we arrived, I had sat in the back seat while Terri sat in the passenger seat. Since the back seat was now gone, the only place for me to sit was inside the refrigerator box. I had to lie down in the box about five-miles to my home. I forgot to mention that I'm very, claustrophobic.

The weekend after Thanksgiving we were allowed to put up our stage extenders, and leave the larger props as long as they didn't interfere with Mass. We met Donnie Steadman, the new owner of Sunco Productions, which happened to be a high school classmate from Mainland Sr. High. At the church, along with his crew, we hung the theatrical lights. The lighting director helped us zero the lights in on each stage closer to production.

Practicing with multiple groups separately made it hard to see the full picture. However, once the actors donned their costumes, everything fell into place. Now, I needed to meet with Chiquita, the church secretary, to advertise the performances in the newspaper and prepare the playbills for distribution.

The weekend preceding the production, following Sunday Mass, marked the final dress rehearsal. It was during this time that all elements cohesively integrated, generating intense sense of anticipation. Each public performance demonstrated continual improvement. Fr. O'Leary observed his congregation, along with the residents of the City of Port Orange, fostering a strong sense of community.

Attendees traveled from various locations, including Orlando, prompting the Bishop to send a news reporter and her cameraman from the Florida Catholic Magazine. Our production received front-page coverage for several, consecutive years.

The reporter was so impressed, she and her crew came to the Sunday Matinee the first year. While I was talking with her, someone brought to my attention that several area nursing home vans were arriving with their residents. Again, not having the time to deal with this problem I said a small prayer, turned around, and there was Bob, the Head Usher at the 11:00 am Sunday Mass. Sitting with him was his wife and several of his usher friends. They were happy to help and took over the project from that moment on. The scripture, Romans 12:5 "So we, being many, are one body in Christ. . ." came together.

God Used Our Group Within Other Ministries

I'll never forget the first year of our productions, we were taking down the stages when Fr. O'Leary found me in the church and said, "I don't know how you do it, Kathe. You got people to serve in this ministry that I couldn't get motivated to do anything. This is the talk of our church community and town. Let's do an Easter Production."

Like I said earlier, I had no idea what God had in store for our entire church community. We only did the Easter Productions for a couple of years. Our Christmas Productions kept getting larger, and being mostly volunteers with school and jobs, it got too hard to continue with both.

The Director of CCD (Catholic Sunday School) also realized that the students had a better understanding of the scriptures. She called me into her office and wanted us to do a few skits on Social Justice. I discussed the areas she needed addressed and wrote a script. John and I handpicked a small group of actors to help us. Mary and Maggie handled the costumes and props we needed.

We began with a skit of a homeless woman with her small daughter looking through a dumpster on a busy, city street. It showed people of all walks of life ignoring them as they walked past them from both directions. A man dressed as a construction worker was walking behind a businessman. When the woman approached the business man, he pushed her out of his way, and continued walking.

The construction worker, who had passed her earlier, hurried to help her stand up while other people ignored what was happening. They pretended to converse for a moment. The construction worker pointed out the bus stop and walked them to the bench by the sign. He sat beside them on a bench offering the child a candy bar from his lunch box as they conversed. It ended with them standing up pretending to see the oncoming bus. He gave them money for the bus and turned to leave. The child hurried to him and gave him a hug for his kindness with the candy bar still in her hand.

The second was a family kneeling in prayer by the bedside of their grandmother. A doctor and nurse were standing at the head of the bed. A Priest enters giving Grandma 'Last Rights' as the family watched while Jesus slowly appears in the background. As the Priest finished, he stood back with the family while the doctor checked her heart with his stethoscope. He looks at the father, shaking his head. The father picks up the youngest child, walking his family sadly out of the room with the Priest consoling the mother. The doctor and nurse covered Grandma with a blanket before leaving.

But as soon as they were gone, Jesus approached her bedside, gently pulls the blanket away, and assists her in standing. Grandmother expresses joy while walking to heaven with Jesus.

I even had my youngest son Britt, a 3rd Degree Black Belt bring in his Sensei with some of the instructors from the Dojo to teach how to avoid bullies, the importance of staying active and fit, staying away from drugs, and other bad situations facing our youth in schools and off campus.

The class started with some initial Karate Katas. After that, the students were divided into smaller groups and were taught several self-defense techniques to escape from an attacker. Everyone wanted to participate, and it too was a huge success.

Each Year Scripts "Fell Into My Head."

The cast was excited every October to sign up for the year's Christmas Productions. Again, the Music Director ordered the Cantata in the summer, so I had time to listen to it and pray about the script. When I least expected it, the script would simply "fall into my head."

Jim and I often attended our daughter, Keely's and granddaughter Paris' ice-skating recitals in Cocoa Beach. I learned the hard way to bring a pen and notepad, as their performances frequently inspired scripts for the Christmas Cantata. It always felt like Jesus was dictating the script, so quickly that I could barely keep up with Him.

Let me give you one example. Once before Keely's and Paris' performance began, a world-renowned figure skater performed. She entered the ice dressed in a light-green leotard with a single, spiraling, dark-green, scalloped wide-ribbon beginning at her right wrist, winding around her arm, spiraling around her bodice, and down one leg.

A large, white ball was strapped to her right hand which lit up as the house lights dimmed. It signified a lonely pearl deep within the ocean. As she glided on the ice holding the pearl, her performance was amplified with the tempo of the music. I couldn't take my eyes off the pearl as she sped up for jumps or slowed down clutching the pearl to her chest. She finished the dance entering into a fast, spinning spiral holding the globe above her head. As the spiral slowed, the globe descended down her body until she was in the sitting position. As her spin stopped, she laid the pearl on the ice next to her. The house lights shut off until the only thing illuminated was the pearl.

It wasn't coincidence that the cantata I was listening to on the way to Cocoa Beach that year was entitled, 'The Light of Christ.' After watching her performance, the entire script flooded my brain. I didn't watch the beginning of Keely's and Paris' performance because I was busy writing notes for the script.

The opening scene in our production depicted Heaven's Gate with Christ inside holding a round globe to signify 'The Light of Christ.' On stage left, Jesus was surrounded by angels of various ages watching a single angelic ballerina dancing outside the gate.

At the end of the song, she faced Heaven's Gate, gracefully bowing to Jesus while identical twin girls opened the gate for Jesus to exit. As Jesus handed her the globe, it instantly lit symbolizing He is 'The Light of the World.' Jesus spoke for her to rise, waving His hand around the audience, asking her to spread 'The Light of Christ' to the ends of the earth. Christ then returned through Heaven's Gate while she danced with 'The Light of Christ' before passing it to the first angelic dancer standing in the audience just below her on the stage.

Leanne arranged angelic dancers of various ages, positioning them a few feet apart from stage left (house right) down the aisles to the middle of the church, then across the middle aisle to the house left aisle, and up the aisle to stage right (house left). Each angelic dancer would pass 'The Light of Christ' to the next angel until it reached the Nativity Scene on house left.

A solitary, angelic ballerina began dancing around the Nativity Scene. The final dancer from the audience presented her with 'The Light of Christ'. She gracefully danced with the lit globe around the Crèche. Upon reaching the climax of the song, she placed 'The Light of Christ' into the Crèche, respectfully bowing, representing the birth of Emmanuel, God with us.

99

The Florida Catholic Magazine featured this scene on the front page that year. It showed six-year-old identical, twin girls standing beside Jesus inside Heaven's Gate. After the dress rehearsal, the reporter asked for the twins' names, but I couldn't tell them apart and referred her to their mother.

Prayer Led By The Holy Spirit

Our group faced many challenges over the years, but we always found a way through them with prayer. One year proved to be the most difficult for one of the liturgical dancers and myself.

Fr. Ray had asked me if we could perform a small-scale Nativity Scene for the Family Christmas Eve Mass at 6:00 pm. Leanne and I put together a small script using minimal actors. It happened during the only dress rehearsal which was a day before the show. I was standing at the podium watching people entering the church. I noticed one of the middle school age girls along with her mother crying while speaking with Leanne.

Leanne hurried to me informing me that the young girl's aunt had died the day before. It was her mother's sister who lived in town. I had seen her many times attending our productions over the years. They were very close and the family decided she should step away from this show due to her grief.

I informed our group to take their seats, and I would get started in a few minutes. Next, along with Leanne, I hurried to the family. With tears in my eyes, I gave them a hug and gave my heartfelt condolences. Then, I shocked them by admitting that yesterday afternoon my oldest brother had passed away. There was no one else to take my place; not even my new Assistant Director, Dave, felt comfortable. Jim encouraged me that 'the

100

show must go on.' And that Christmas is a time for hope. It is the celebration of the birth of Jesus, who would one day give His life that we may live again.

I glanced at my watch. It was time to begin the practice. I asked them to stay for prayer and slowly approached the Altar, wondering what I was going to say. I remember standing at the podium, and a peace came over me. The Holy Spirit guided me through every word of the prayer. I can't even tell you what I said. But I do know it was powerful. I glanced around the pews and saw tears throughout the audience. I ended with Our Lady of Hope, pray for us.

After the prayer, the young girl and her mother hurried with Leanne to the altar. They gave me a hug, saying that her aunt loved our shows, so she decided to perform. Christ turned our ashes into beauty. It was an unforgettable Christmas Eve Mass. Isaiah 61:3 "To all who mourn in Israel, He will give a crown of beauty for ashes."

Listening to That 'Still Small Voice'

On Valentine's Day two months later, Jim and I attended a Knights of Columbus Dinner and Dance in the Parish Center. We were sitting at a table with friends from the Respect Life Group which I was the Chairman of. It had been a long day, and I was ready for a glass of wine, and an evening of dancing with Jim and friends. Father Ray had just welcomed everyone and said the prayer for our meal.

We had just gotten a glass of wine and sat down with some hors d'oeuvres as the lights lowered, and the music began.

The lights from the disco ball hanging from the ceiling set the mood of the song from the eighties. Everyone was having a good time.

One of the couples from the Christmas Production said hello to us as they passed our table on the way to the dance floor. They were 'snowbirds' that lived in upstate New York and came to Florida to get away from the harsh winters. Now years later, as I recall one of God's warnings through The Holy Spirit, I can't remember their names.

As they entered the dance floor, I noticed they were dancing under the disco ball. As I took my first sip of wine, I heard very strongly in my head, "put the wine down now." I even leaned over to Jim whispering what happened. He, too, put his glass of wine down and we drank water with our hors d'oeuvres.

For some reason, my eyes kept glancing at the disco ball, noticing it was right over my friend's head. The song ended and another song began with nothing happening. But for some reason, I couldn't take my eyes off that object. Then, I suddenly felt it was going to fall. I had a strong feeling that I should tell them to move, but before I could stand up, the disco ball dropped on top of his head.

He fell straight down as a board not bending his knees or hitting his butt first. His head bounced on the floor. But suddenly he jumped back up and started to dance again. Then, he fell unconscious to the floor. Several of the doctors in the room ran over to him, including Jim. Someone called 911. The Fire Station with the EMT's was a half a block away.

I hurried over to be with his wife while the EMT's worked with him, before putting him on a stretcher. His wife asked to ride with them in the ambulance. They told her that she might get in the way and to meet them at the nearby hospital on Dunlawton Avenue.

This is why I wasn't supposed to drink my wine. God knows I drive a Corvette and have a lead foot. I knew his wife was in shock, so I told Jim to drive her and that I would follow them. We had parked in the front of the church, and it took me a few minutes to join them at the hospital. When I arrived, Jim and the victim's wife were joined by another EMT rushing to join them from a second ambulance. It was evident that he knew them.

When Jim got back in the 'vette with me, he explained that the EMT was their son. He had heard the call come into dispatch for an ambulance needed at OLOH's Parish Center along with the patient's name. He was working in another part of town. As soon as he heard the call, the driver drove him straight to meet them.

As we drove back to the church to have dinner, we prayed for them, and thanked God for warning me not to drink. Again, when that 'still small voice' warns you not to do something, it is always for a reason. The disco ball had been in the ceiling for years with no problems. God warned me that it would fall, and I needed to be ready to drive. If we go out for an evening and have drinks, Jim always drives home. That's also the reason why I couldn't take my eyes off the disco ball sensing it was going to fall.

That Still Small Voice Warned Again

It wasn't long after that when I had another warning by The Holy Spirit. It was in the wee hours of the morning. Jim and I were sound asleep. Two of our sons, Zachary and Britt were living in the house with us at the time. We awoke to our burglar alarm

103

blaring throughout the house. Jim grabbed his gun as I checked the panel in our bedroom which read exterior garage door open. We hurried to the hallway in the middle of the house leading to the interior garage door. Zachary, and Britt met us from the other side of the house.

Jim turned on the garage and outside lights as he opened the interior, garage door. He glanced around the cars, but not in between them, before noticing the exterior door was still ajar. He and the boys went outside to look around as ADT asked me if I still needed the police deployed. I was on speakerphone, so anyone could hear us.

At first, I didn't see anything unusual as I looked around inside the garage, since Jim left the door wide open. In my head I kept hearing, 'deploy the police,' so I complied. ADT told me they would stay on the line with me until the police arrived. While Jim and the boys were outside, I had backed away from the garage door into the opening of the hallway closest to the kitchen. At a glance, I could see the long hallway to the back part of the house, and also through the dining room into our bedroom.

When Jim and the boys finally came back inside the house, Jim closed the external garage door and locked it before entering the hallway. He then locked the interior garage door. I explained to dispatch what was happening. Since Jim and the boys didn't see anything unusual, dispatch asked me again, if I wanted to cancel the police. Our alarm panel showed that now we had a green light. I asked Jim, and he thought it would be okay. But in my head, The Holy Spirit kept telling me to 'deploy the police.' So, I said, "No, send the police. Something is not right."

The next thing we all saw on the alarm panel was the green light went off for a few seconds, then came back on as we heard the external garage door slam closed. Clearly someone had just left our garage! Jim and the boys stayed inside until the police arrived.

Some of the officers checked around outside as we talked with an officer who came to the front door. We told the officer the story about what just happened on the alarm panel. He said that we were lucky that I did not cancel the police. There had been a rash of home invasions in the area. It sounded like the invader was lying either under one of the cars or close enough that Jim didn't see him. He was listening to everything I said. If we would have canceled them, he would have attacked us.

That's when I realized I was standing in the hallway with the interior, garage door wide open the entire time Jim and the boys were outside. If I hadn't been on the phone with ADT, the invader could have grabbed me and had a gun to my head when they came back. Our family would have been in grave danger, and we would have been robbed.

A Third Warning in a Row

A third time, which happened right in a row, I was protected by The Holy Spirit again. I had been at a production meeting held at the costume designer's house not far from my home. Jim was home and on the phone with one of our children. Britt was also home, since I noticed his car was in the driveway.

When I turned the corner to our street, I noticed an old, yellow Cadillac parked off the side of the road by the neighbor just before my driveway. As I pulled into the driveway, I glanced in my rearview mirror before I opened the garage door. That's when I noticed the Cadillac had pulled across my driveway sideways and stopped. A black man had gotten out and was walking towards my house. At first, I pushed the garage door opener, and it began opening. That's when I heard in my head, "close the garage door." I pushed the button closing it and tried to call Jim for help. The line was still busy and he wasn't changing lines.

By this time, the gentleman was standing even with my car door. I lowered the window a quarter of the way, and asked, "Can I help you?"

The man said that he was selling books to put himself through college.

I immediately answered, "No thank you. I have four children in college that I'm helping."

He asked me the same thing again and I gave him the same answer. But he did not want to accept the answer. I pushed redial on my phone, but the line was still busy.

Finally, he threw his hands up in the air and yelled, "just give me some money!"

That's when I noticed his eyes shift for a second to my purse on the seat next to me. That's when The Holy Spirit warned, "Put your car in reverse. If he tries to reach inside the window, step on the gas." Next, I was told to, "Rev up the engine," which I immediately did. That action sent a clear message to the man, and he left. I checked my rearview mirror, and saw him running, not walking to his car.

After, he drove away, I backed down the driveway and made sure he left our street. Then, I drove inside the garage, closed the garage door, hurried inside the dining room, and called the police. Jim was still on the phone in the kitchen but got off when he heard me talking with the police. Within five minutes two police cars were in the area. One parked at the street in front of our house. I noticed the other car slowly looking around the wooded areas of the houses next door.

The officer wanted a full description of the car and man. He said that two of these men had been reported working the Port Orange area. They had been on alert for them, since it was reported that they were getting more aggressive to people. He said that seemed to be the case with me. Now, they needed to intensify the search. If I saw the car again, I was to report it to the police immediately.

Chapter Fourteen

Understanding The Lady at the Well

Easter seemed to come very early that year. In the three-year cycle of the Liturgical Calendar on the third week of Easter, the Lady at the Well was featured from the Gospel of John 4:7-31. Since the Christmas Productions were a great ministry tool in teaching the gospel, Father Ray asked me if I would perform The Lady at the Well during the Homily. It was a great honor. However, it was one scripture I did not understand – yet, that is.

In preparing the script, again I turned to James 1:5 "If any of you lacks wisdom, let him ask God, who gives to all men generously and without reproaching, and it will be given him."

In my research, I read the opinions of several Biblical Scholars. As I read John Chapter Four over and over, I got chills understanding the goodness of God, whereas nothing is coincidence with Him. Every moment in our lives is already planned out to the tiniest detail. It's how we choose to listen to Him and answer His call that matters. When I said that I didn't understand the scripture, yet that is. I had no clue how much this scripture would impact my personal life.

Jesus went out of His way to go to Jacob's Well, precisely at the right time of day to seek the Samaritan Woman. One thing that jumped out at me was she reminded me of (Hebrews 11:6). "And without Faith it is impossible to please Him. For whoever would draw near to God must believe that He exists and that He rewards those who seek Him." She had an insatiable yearning for seeking the Messiah.

The Lady at the Well symbolizes all Christians and Jews who seek the Messiah. For without Jesus and His Eternal Peace, we have no peace, no hope, no happiness. Outside of Mary, Joseph, and the Twelve Disciples that made up His immediate circle, the Lady at the Well is the first-person Jesus told that He was the Messiah. Where and how He chose to tell her was monumental in bringing the entire village to know that Jesus is the Messiah.

Although not named in the scriptures, this woman's story significantly illustrates the extent to which Jesus is willing to go to save each individual who earnestly seeks Him. It was an honor to portray her on the Altar of Christ, complete with providing me a humbling experience.

The Lady at the Well further signifies God's love for all mankind and that He is willingly to redeem us no matter what our circumstance may be. She was a female in a society where women were demeaned and disregarded, and from a race traditionally despised by Jews. She was known in town for going from man to man because their love could not satisfy her. Ultimately, everything they offered her was not the kind of love her heart was yearning.

It was usually the custom for women to go to Jacob's Well in groups early in the morning to avoid the heat and for safety of predators. As a social outcast, the women in town shunned her. So, she always went alone at the noon hour in the heat of the day. Jacob's Well would be empty of that judging crowd.

She always carried her empty vessel, but the fact is, she was the empty vessel. Nothing and no one could satisfy her heart.

It was an intangible emotion that she wanted, something she needed, something she must have, but something she couldn't have. Until one day, a day she would never forget, nor the generations after generations that would precede her.

Little did she know that day her quest would be fulfilled. Jesus and His disciples left Judea to depart again into Galilee. Jesus purposely wanted to pass through Samaria to a city called Sychar even though His disciples offered easier routes to Galilee. When they reached Jacob's Well, Jesus sent the disciples into town to get something to eat while he waited alone in the shade by the well.

To her astonishment when she arrived noticing a Jewish man sitting in the shade, she boldly decided to ignore Him. And what happened next was even more astonishing! He, a Jewish man spoke to her, a Samaritan woman, "woman, give me drink . . ."

To bring this scripture to life I needed specific props. I asked the carpenters to build me a working well. So, I could draw water from the well and pour it into a jar. We placed it in the center of the altar. Another prop I needed was the small stage placed out into the middle of house right's pews. This represented the store in town where some townspeople of all ages shopped and where the disciples went to buy food.

Again, that small stage and having characters walk through the aisles pulls the audience more into the storyline.

I began the performance in a small room behind the altar on house-right with a monologue about the struggles of my life before entering the set and slowly walking towards Jacob's Well. I would stop, set my large jar down, and wipe my forehead as Jesus and His disciples entered from the sacristy in back from house left.

Of course, they were mic'd as they talked, slowly walking along the way about an easier route to Galilee. Matthew even pulled out his map proving to Jesus the way through Sychar was clearly miles out of their way. And showing Him the route that would take hours off the trip. But Jesus insisted they travel through Sychar, so they continued through the heat of the day towards their destiny.

When Jesus and the disciples finally approached Jacob's Well, Jesus immediately sent them to town for food. It was Peter who insisted on staying with Jesus to protect Him, but Jesus assured Peter that He would be fine. As they later would learn and understand, Jesus had a specific mission to do alone. The disciples walked around the aisles to the town pretending to converse and then pretended to greet the store owner to purchase food.

That is when I walked with my empty vessel to Jacob's Well, ignoring the man sitting beside it as I drew water a couple of times, carefully pouring it into my jar. That is until He spoke to me. That is when I straightened up and turned towards Him. It was obvious that she was not afraid of talking with men, so I portrayed her as feisty, willing to boldly question Jesus about the water He wanted me to give Him. Then, He offered me Living Water so I would never thirst again. At the part where Jesus asked me to go and bring my husband, emotions welled up inside me.

It was at that moment that the Spirit of The Lady at the Well felt like she was with me. I felt emotions on that Altar that I had never felt while practicing my lines at home. Suddenly, I had a hard time giving Jesus eye contact and felt ashamed of who I was. I began whispering to myself about how unsatisfied my life was, leaning my head on the top of The Well, while running my fingers over the top of the rim, breathing deeply as if His words cut through my very soul. I found myself struggling to answer Jesus feeling ashamed of what I had done. After a moment, I finally mustard enough courage to whisper, "I have no husband." That is when Jesus said that I was right, and that I had had five husbands, and the man I was living with wasn't my husband.

To my surprise, my sins felt like they were lifted as He spoke those words. Then, I fell back into my character, reciting the rest of the script as I talked with Jesus concerning whether He was a prophet. That is when Jesus talked about the Living Water that only He could give me, and I would never thirst again. . . How it would be better than our ancestor's water in Jacob's Well that he, his family, and animals drank from. My lines continued with John 4:25, 26. "I know the Messiah is coming, He who is called the Christ; when He comes, He will show us all things." Jesus answered me, "I who speak to you, am He."

At that moment, I was humbled and excited at the same time, that Jesus sought me, a Samaritan Woman, a social outcast to tell that He was the Messiah, until I noticed His friends joining us, looking at me as if I had some nerve conversing with Him. For a moment, the shame that the Lady at the Well must have felt, came over me again as I heard them whispering amongst themselves.

I glanced back to Jesus and felt free again, bravely sharing my witness to them that Jesus told me He is the Messiah. That must have been so overwhelming to her. The scriptures say that is when she ran past them straight to the people in town that she had always avoided, crying, "Come and see, come, and see, the Man that told me everything I have ever done! He told me He is the Messiah."

Imagine her running back to those who once shunned her, now empowered by the Holy Spirit to convince them to follow her to Jacob's Well. The scripture says in verses 40-42: "When the Samaritans came to Him, they asked Him to stay with them; He stayed for two days. Many more believed because of His word. They said to the woman, 'It is no longer because of your words that we believe, but because we have heard for ourselves and know that He is the Savior of the world.'"

At the end of the performance, the Lady at the Well was to sprinkle Holy Water on the congregation and sing as she did it. But since I do not sing, I asked a good friend of mine to sing for me. OLOH was honored to have a guest singer, Rob Rock, perform during all three Masses.

Two years ago, Rob was inducted into the Music Hall of Fame. I couldn't put the video of the performance on my website, and neither could Rob, since the pianist 'the problem' decided to sabotage me one last time. Instead of playing the sheet music, 'the problem' decided to hit a few keys now and then. However, Rob knew the situation and sang wonderfully with the fantastic, range of his voice 'A Cappella'. After previewing the video, Rob didn't want it on his website or mine since the pianist was so rude.

It was a fantastic memory for me to have the honor to perform on stage with Rob Rock.

Father Ray was thrilled with the entire performance. He couldn't believe how well my performance portrayed her character, and, neither could I! After my last performance at the Sunday 11:00 am Mass, a CCD Teacher actually approached me admitting that she never understood that scripture until I brought it to life. She shared that the emotions I portrayed were so surreal, it was as if she was in the village crowd listening to The

113

Lady at the Well tell her story. I had to confess that it was an extraordinary experience for me.

Chapter Fifteen

Divine Strength During a Crisis

In September of 2001, what awaited our church community as well as our country only God knew, and it shook the very core of every American. Five months after the Easter performance on September 11, 2001, about eight o'clock in the morning, two hijacked airliners filled with passengers and its crew, piloted by Islamic Terrorists, struck New York City's Twin Towers. A third airliner that struck the Pentagon Building. A fourth airliner was on course to crash into the Capitol Building in Washington, DC. The terrorists aboard that airliner allowed passengers to use their cell phones to call their loved ones to insight more terror.

Upon learning of the fate of the other three airliners, the brave passengers of Flight #93 foiled the last jet from hitting the Capitol Building by overcoming the terrorist causing it to crash in a field in Pennsylvania. Over 3,000 people were murdered that day on American soil.

The Christmas Production was the last thing on our minds. Until Father Ray met with Mary and I expressing our ministry was needed now more than ever. He said that the way we brought the scriptures to life would help our parishioners feel 'The Hope' that Christmas brings to the world.

As I pondered the script, for some reason one of the many characters the famed comedian, Red Skelton, performed during my childhood strongly stuck in my mind. It was as if God was telling me that our community needed to laugh again. The clown Freddie the Freeloader was only a mime, but he made people of all ages laugh. One memorable performance involved him miming, taking a piece of thread out of his pants pocket, a needle out of his shirt pocket, and sewing his fingers together. He then pretended to pull the string casting shadows on the wall resembling animals.

I wrote a special script called "Back to Our Town." Now that I think about it, the title depicted how American's felt at that time. The main character, so-called Freddie the Freeloader, wanted his hometown of New York City and our country back to safety and peace that has always been in America. A peace, even after years later, every American would still long for but never see again.

As the story unfolded, a newspaper reporter from New York City was continually covering stories about the emergency and volunteer crews still sifting through the ruble of The Twin Towers, and our Military fighting this evil abroad by chasing down the terrorists. His wife was nagging him that he wasn't home anymore, and even when he was there his mind was somewhere else. His boss was yelling at him that he couldn't write articles fast enough and he needed to be on the next flight oversees for Realtime Coverage.

Overwhelmed, exhausted, and depressed, from traveling abroad, his mind kept wandering back to his childhood safe place. A quaint, Southern town nestled in the mountains of North Carolina where he camped and fished with his grandfather. Since his grandfather had passed, he hadn't been back.

Early one morning, instead of boarding a plane for abroad at Kennedy Airport, he bought a ticket to go to his grandfather's house. He chuckled thinking about cooking fish on an open fire and sleeping in a tent as he took his seat. As his phone started to ring, he powered it down, placed it deep in his duffle bag, and pushed it under the seat. Then, he closed his eyes as the plane took off reminiscing of his childhood.

When he arrived, he found his grandfather's house was now a small General Store/Post Office. Not wanting to interact with the townspeople too much, he realized he needed supplies. Hesitantly, he entered the store quickly picking up a can opener, bread, can of tuna, and a fishing pole before heading to the lake. The owner tried to make small talk by asking him if he needed a place to stay and how long he would be in town. Avoiding her questions, he simply answered that he wasn't sure as he paid and left. But everyone who entered the store that day heard about the stranger in town, including the mayor, and chief of police. Madison, a five-year-old, shopping with her grandmother and two siblings was also among the shoppers that day.

I chose a father with his five-year-old daughter duo, and they were a smash hit. His wife was the store owner, so all their interactions were natural. They had plenty of time to practice their lines. It worked out great. Back to the storyline.

The first night he was in town as Madison's grandmother was listening to her bedtime prayers, Madison asked her grandmother about the stranger. Madison's grandmother had told her that the police deemed him harmless. But then, Grandma adds that he's just a 'Freddie the Freeloader' Type. He sleeps on a bench in the park. He's a lazy person that doesn't care about anyone or anything. She further explained to Madison that all he needed to be happy was to find the hope that only Jesus can give.

After grandmother tucks Madison in bed and leaves the room, she hurries to her window. Getting on her knees, she boldly prays to Heavenly Father to make Freddy fall off the bench, hit his head, and find Jesus. All was quiet as she fell asleep.

117

Except, God answering Madison's prayer by sending an overzealous angel the next morning to shape him up, in a very unconventional manner. . . let's just say this angel had attitude!

I have to admit, I got the idea of the 'angel with attitude' from the 1988 movie with Bill Murray as 'Scrooge'. Carol Kane portrayed the Angel of Christmas Present as unpredictable and feisty as an angel could be.

Our show was just what our parishioners, along with the community needed to rekindle the Christmas Spirit of Hope, which God the Father gave us with the birth of His Only Begotten Son, Jesus Christ.

This production led to our parishioners anticipating with excitement the sign-ups for next year's show. I also noticed an influx of parishioners having babies born between October to December, each wanting their baby to play Baby Jesus. We were always blessed with a newborn so we could switch out babies if one became cranky. That is, all but the last year; I should clarify that no one from OUR PARISH had a baby. But as we found out, nothing stops what God ordained to happen.

God's Divine Plan

That summer, Leanne's family faced a terrible tragedy, and they didn't feel like attending church, much less working on a musical. Leanne suggested that I find a replacement. However, again I was filled with the Holy Spirit as we talked, and she agreed to continue with the show.

Reflecting on challenging years, it's clear how God works through others. Take Frank Speck, a retired baker from up north, as an example of God's plan. When he and his wife Dorothy brought their grandchildren to audition for a play, I needed more adult actors. I asked Frank and Dorothy if the wanted to join the cast. Frank almost cried, saying no one had ever asked him to participate in anything before.

From that moment on, they never missed a practice and were always on time. I'll never forget a few days after the shows were over that first year, Frank called me while I was on the way to take some costumes back to the rental store. He said, "Miss Kathe, I'm so depressed now that the shows are over." I told Frank that it was normal to feel that way after being in the limelight, but the more he performs the easier it gets. I told him that he did a great job, and I looked forward to him signing up again.

The last year I directed, the Cantata included the scene from the Gospel of Luke 2:25-35 about Simeon, the old Prophet who couldn't die until he saw the Christ Child. When it came time to cast the parts, Frank stood out in my mind for the part of Simeon. Let's say even though Frank had performed several years in a row, he always required a little TLC to give him the confidence he needed.

He was so excited that I picked him to play the character of Simeon. When I handed him a script, I watched him eagerly running his finger down the script reading through the lines. He looked at me wide-eyed and in shock gasping, "It's a speaking role." I remember telling Frank that he was ready.

A few days before we went to the three-day production, Frank was still struggling to remember his few lines. I had Dorothy and Frank meet me one afternoon at church to work with him on stage. I'll never forget, we went over his line's multiple times, but Frank kept stumbling.

Finally, he said, "Miss Kathe, I can't do it." Then, Dorothy loving swatted him saying, "Oh, Frank, even the sheep know your lines!"

Maggie Greene was working on last minute touches to the props on stage left. I asked her if she could join us. A few people were in the church, so we went into the room behind the altar on stage left. There was one chair in the middle of the room like it was waiting for us. It was odd, because I had been in that room many times and there was never a chair. I asked Frank to sit, explaining that I was going to give him a Blessing of Mother Mary, which Fr. M. J. Joachim Tierney gave me the power to perform years earlier at the Monastery in Conyers, GA. So, Maggie, Dorothy, and I put our hands on his head.

As Catholic's we believe in the Communion of Saints. Matthew 18:20 "For where two or three are gathered in My Name, there am I in the midst of them." The Holy Spirit was truly with us that afternoon when we gave Frank the blessing. I can't take any credit for that blessing. It wasn't me that gave it. Before I knew it, I said, "even Simeon, Himself would help Frank remember his lines and give him the confidence he needs to bring this scripture to life." After the blessing, we went home and didn't see each other until the Friday Night Show.

Frank's wife, Dorothy played Anna, the Prophetess who didn't leave the Temple. Luke 2:34-35 The Holy Spirit prompted Simeon to go to the Temple, the day Mary and Joseph brought Jesus to be dedicated to the Lord. Simeon's mountain was located out into the audience in front of stage right.

When the music began, he was to walk down the steps, put on his sandals, cloak, and take his staff on the journey across the middle aisle over to house left where the Temple Scene was set. He was to take off his cloak, sandals, and leave his staff

120

before entering the Temple and kneel next to Anna. He was to keep praying as other couples entered with their babies. However, when Mary holding Jesus with Joseph entered, he was to rush to her and take the Child Jesus in his arms, hold Him up, and cry, "Now I can die for I have seen the Christ Child, the Messiah, the Savior of the World, etc." Then, Anna was to give a blessing to the Christ Child, and also to Mary.

Frank was in his late seventies and not steady enough to hold a baby toward heaven, so I arranged for the High Priest to have his hands under the child for safety. Friday and Saturday evening shows went as I had planned. But that's not what happened at the Sunday Matinee! As I have said before, several things were already in motion to happen within a short couple of weeks.

Let me rewind to the week earlier. Remember our parish didn't have a small baby born that year. It was also the year that Jim's brother from Utah and his family wanted to visit us, so they could watch a Christmas Production. That meant coming the weekend after Thanksgiving weekend. I remember sitting by Jim's side on the computer planning the dates of the trip with them.

But as fate would have it, Jim and his brother switched the tickets to Thanksgiving weekend without telling me after I left the room. Even though I made it perfectly clear to everyone on the phone. Thanksgiving weekend, I have to set up the stage for production. The weekend I MUST be at church as writer/director to make sure everything was set in the precise spot to coincide with the lightning.

Jim and his brother had also planned for us to visit St. Augustine and tour Flagler College where one of our daughter's attended. I reminded Jim multiple times that he knew that

121

weekend didn't work for me, and to change the tickets to the next weekend. But he couldn't and I was stuck! That was also the weekend that my assistant director's daughter was moving to college, and he had to be out of town helping her and he couldn't get out of it either.

But all was not lost, and God had something very special in mind for my side-trip to St. Augustine. When I went down to the church to find someone to take over, Leanne was frantic standing on the Altar of Christ. I'll never forget her saying, "I knew I should have never agreed to do this show. Now you can't be here when we need you the most, and we don't even have a Baby Jesus. What are we going to do?"

I looked her straight in the eyes, and said, "You know what I need to handle this set up for me. I don't want you to worry about not having a Baby Jesus; I'll worry about it." That's when I realized we were standing on the Altar of Christ and said, "I'm not going to worry about it, I'll let God worry about it." Then, I looked around the altar at all the people and props and said, "God's not worried about it. When we least expect it, God will give us a Baby Jesus!" And I left.

Notice the words I said standing on the Altar of Christ. Luke 7:1-10 tells the story of the Roman Centurion's sick servant's son that was dying and the words he had his elders say to Jesus. "Lord do not trouble Yourself, for I am not worthy that You should enter under my roof. Therefore, I did not even think myself worthy to come to You. But say the word, and my servant's son will be healed." This is the only time, the scriptures said that Jesus 'marveled' at the Centurion's faith. "When Jesus heard these things, He marveled at him and turned around and said to the crowd that followed Him, 'I say to you, I have not found such great faith, not even in Israel.'

As God planned it, Jim's brother and family left our house before, I got back home from church. Jim had to loan his car to our youngest son, whose car broke down, so we took my Corvette. Jim and his brother were supposed to meet at the Volusia Mall, then they would follow us. Without breakfast and now it was almost lunch time, they never showed up. Every time Jim would call, they stalled us by making excuses.

Later, we found out they stopped at a restaurant and ate, while we were waiting to eat with them. Our daughter at Flagler College was waiting for us to show up, so we had to push the time back with her a couple of times due to a few more stops along the way.

Finally, Jim and I decided to leave without his brother, but as soon as I got on I-95 N., I noticed I needed gas. I stopped at a truck stop along the way. When we got back on I-95 N. traffic was dead stopped in both directions.

Jim called his brother, and they were two miles ahead of us now, so we told them to take the next exit and meet us on A1A, heading toward Marineland. Jim's brother was raised in Ormond Beach and knew the area. That's when his brother said that he read online that Marineland was free since they were doing some renovations.

So, we stopped again at Marineland since his family had never seen a dolphin. As we were walking up a walkway over the Dolphin Exhibit, a woman with a newborn baby and two toddlers were even with us on the lower level. We got to talking and for some reason I boldly said, "I'm directing a church Christmas Production and this year we didn't have any babies born to play Baby Jesus. She asked me what date the show was, and I shared all three dates. Then, I said, "but I don't live anywhere near here."

She then said the same thing. Then, she said she lived in Port Orange. My heart leaped out of my body as I said, "so do I!"

I asked her if she knew where Our Lady of Hope Catholic Church on Clyde Morris was located. She said that she was a working mother, and that the church across the street was her daycare. Her husband agreed that those dates worked for them. I told her that we could put the newborn's brothers on the Nativity Stage dressed as sheep, and that we filmed the shows. That made it perfect, and they were Catholic thinking about coming back to Catholic Church.

The funny thing was, neither of us had paper and pen, so she had a crayon in her diaper bag, and I had a napkin to exchange names and numbers. On the way to St. Augustine College, I called Leanne and told her the good news. Next, I called Mary and told her that we had not only a Baby Jesus but two sheep for her to dress. The next day, the family showed up for the last dress rehearsal, and I gave them a script.

Another side note, the mother of Baby Jesus was a nurse. She adopted at birth each of her three sons. She had taken two weeks off to be with their new son. Her husband that afternoon was supposed to take the two older boys for a haircut with him. By that morning, they were sick of being stuck in the house, so they went for a ride up A1A to have lunch at a well-known restaurant. They met several bikers inside with their wives and started talking while having a few beers. They realized they couldn't drive home, and they were a few blocks from Marineland, so they stopped there to clear their heads.

What were the odds? Look what God orchestrated to get all of us from Port Orange to Marineland at the exact time! It was no coincidence that they chose to stay on the ground level at the same time we chose to use the catwalk to the second level and

124

stopped even with each other. Nor was it a coincidence, that I heard that 'still small voice' in my heard prompting me to strike up a conversation about directing a production and needing a Baby Jesus. None of us were supposed be anywhere near there! Coincidence is God's way of staying anonymous!

Back to Simeon at the Sunday Matinee. Everything was going as planned. When it came time for Simeon to leave his mountain and go to the Temple, he followed my instructions as he did on Friday and Saturday nights with the High Priest helping him hold up Baby Jesus. During the Sunday Matinee, Simeon entered as before and knelt by Anna. Mary, Jesus, and Jospeh entered right on time. But what happened next almost gave me a heart attack!

Simeon glanced over his shoulder, saw Mary with Jesus, rushed over to them, took the two-week-old baby in his arms, walked a few steps away from the High Priest, held Baby Jesus up towards heaven, and with amazing emotion said his lines. It was done with such confidence I almost cried and told my stage managers on headsets that it was his best performance. Then, Simeon gave Baby Jesus back to Mary and left the Temple in the same manner he came. He went back on his mountain. At the crescendo of the music, I stood up, pretending to slit my throat with my hand. That was Franks cue to die. He actually fell down this time in a dramatic style.

Later, after the show I went backstage to see if Frank was hurt. He was standing next to the parents holding Baby Jesus. The mother told me that she worked with Frank and helped him feel comfortable holding the baby.

But what Frank told me with a confident gleam in his eyes, I will never forget. "Miss Kathe, it was as if Simeon, Himself was with me holding Baby Jesus. I had the confidence to step away from the High Priest, hold Baby Jesus up towards the heavens, and say my lines! It was exactly like you said when you gave me the Blessing of Mary."

Later, I realized it was God's gift to me to end my career at Our Lady of Hope as writer/director. As miraculous as how God called me to do the productions, it ended with a miraculous finish.

Chapter Sixteen

Even Jesus Was Betrayed

By the next summer, Fr. Raymond O'Leary had retired, and a new priest was assigned to the parish.

Another very important fact I never really addressed was that God always surrounded our production team with His much-needed protection.

At the very infancy of God's idea for bringing His gospel to life on His Altar, He knew who I would be up against. Jesus protected us from the church's main sniveling back-biter. It was very heartbreaking for me to realize that someone can work for a church because it's only another paycheck to them. To me, I was chosen to serve the Lord my God, and church community.

This person only wanted things his way and had already run off several parishioners before me. He was fired from another area church for doing the same thing. When God calls you to do something, always trust in Him. The scriptures are filled with many verses on trusting in the Lord. In this case, Proverbs 29:25 comes to my mind. "Fear of man will prove to be a snare, but whoever trusts in the Lord is kept safe."

I learned the hard way that each time I drove to the church during practices or productions was to call upon St. Michael to protect us, St. Raphael to keep us healthy and St. Gabriel to give us the Mighty Voice of God.

One of the first things that comes to my mind was the 'missing microphone episode.' I was accused by this person of stealing a handheld microphone to Fr. Ray and the office staff. One of my major allies knew the person well and what he was capable of doing. He went into that person's private office, found the microphone in the bottom drawer of a locked filing cabinet underneath a book. God knows every minute detail in a person's life, and no one can hide the truth from Him.

During the first couple of years, an elderly parishioner who was acting on stage with us, turned a hundred-years-old during her last performance. She was a very active and feisty, little lady and never missed a line or cue. She only asked me one time if she could miss a practice. The nursing home where she lived was giving her birthday party. I'll also never forget at her very first practice, I went to help her up the steps to stage left, and she slapped my hand, and said, "I can do it myself."

Two years later, as I was almost ready to go to headsets, my ally brought to my attention that she was in the audience sitting not far from me. My assistant director and I had just finished the lighting and sound checks. So we all hurried over to greet her.

We talked for a few minutes with her as she handed me an envelope. She said this is for me to read after the show. When we turned around to go back to our stations, we saw 'our problem' walk out of the sacristy where the sound system was located. He stood behind the last row of pews, crossing his arms, rocking back and forth on its heels, grinning like a Cheshire Cat, and looking around the packed church.

Instantly, 'that still small voice' inside my head said, 'the sound system is off.' My ally and assistant director also noticed him. We all said at the same time, "the sound system." My assistant director ran to the sacristy, and the door was locked, he went to get a hidden key close by, and it was gone. My ally had to run to his office in another building and get the key to open it. Sure, enough the sound system had been turned off. After the three shows that year, John my Assistant Director gave his notice.

128

He couldn't handle someone that worked for the church constantly trying to sabotage what we were doing.

Oh, and after the show, I read the letter in the envelope. She said, "I'll be with Jesus soon, and I'll whisper in His ear a good word for you." I still have that letter to this day.

Her letter reminded me of another letter I was given a copy of from one of the staff members. It was addressed to 'the problem' in the office. The letter read to the effect that one of our parishioners is a Dean at a College. Every year, he has to sit and watch Campus Christmas Productions as part of his job. Yet, in 2001 watching 'Back to Our Town' after 911, with the newspaper reporter who the town called, 'Freddie the Freeloader,' he said he was thoroughly entertained. He further stated, it was a fresh idea and very well done. It was as if he was watching a Broadway Show in New York City. Of course, 'the problem' didn't want me to see it. I'm thankful that the staff member gave me a copy. I still have a copy of that letter too.

Plotted Against And Blindsided

The summer after that very successful Christmas Production with Simeon, and Baby Jesus, I found myself listening to Christmas music on the beach of all places. The song, 'Carol of the Bells' with the original lyrics caught my attention. In my Corvette on the way home I listened to the song in surround sound. A script began to 'fall into my head' as I visualized placing two small groups of the choir members dressed as angels in each corner in the back of the church and two groups in the front of the church at house left and right. That would give it the surround sound of angels caroling from different directions.

When I got home, I started the outline of the show. I couldn't get the song out of my head for days. I learned the lyrics and walked around the house singing it. It was a great song to showcase the talent of our choir, orchestra, and production team to the new priest.

I told my friend Jean about the idea, and she loved it. She went with me the next morning to early morning Mass to meet the priest and introduce myself. After Mass, I introduced myself to him and was totally blindsided by his response. He said that the production was already way underway. He said I was sent an email explaining a new director had taken over. Jean and I left church in disbelief and shock.

When I got home, I read the email in horror and disbelief with tears streaming down my cheeks. I had been replaced. During that year, Jim and I had hired a new parishioner and his wife to remodel our kitchen. Of course he hadn't passed the test for a Contractor's License, but we trusted him to do a good job. I thought back to the last days they were working in my home. For months, while we were at work, these were the very people I had trusted with my alarm code and free reign inside my home. I remembered that his wife told me that she had a degree in theater and stage lighting. She thought the plays should take on a new direction. I reminded her that our productions were the talk of the town and that things were going great.

What God knew, and I didn't was 'the problem' never wanted actors in the productions. He only wanted the choir and orchestra. Even with all the many years of the success. He waited until the retirement of Fr. Ray to make his move. When the new priest was assigned, he and the woman who designed my kitchen, devised a way to get rid of me. The way the 'so-called elites' of the church fired me after all the years I freely gave my time, and talent was so cruel, I didn't step a foot in that church for years.

But they were chosen by God to do the productions. 'The New Professional Theater and Lighting Director,' and the Choir Director did it their own way. I was told it flopped big-time! The entire Church Community was upset. People walked out of the show. The second year my Assistant Director, Dave, agreed to take 'The Professional Theater and Lighting Director's' place along with the Assistant Music Director taking the Choir Director's place. It flopped also.

What God knew and I didn't was that two of the 'so-called elites' had taken the new priest under their wings and painted his rectory when he arrived. They also took him to City Island Baseball Games. In politics, it's called 'pay for play', but in church it's called 'backstabbing.' Whenever I got upset, God kept reminding me of all the joy, we as a Church Community, brought to the parishioners, and residents of Port Orange.

What God knew, and the 'so called elites' didn't care was when it first happened, my thoughts immediately turned to Frank and Leanne. Knowing who the 'so-called elites' were, they wouldn't give Frank the TLC that I did. And Leanne and her dancers weren't wanted either, so I did call them to let them know the truth about what happened.

When I called Frank and Dorothy and told them that I wasn't going to do the production, Frank told me that the first day of sign-ups he asked where I was. They told him that I didn't want to do the shows anymore. Frank knew it was a lie and walked away brokenhearted and disgusted. Some of our other crew members changed churches because they knew what we went through behind the scenes.

I happened to run into the Head Usher, Bob and his wife, in Walmart one night. He said the first year it was so bad, that people walked out of the show shaking their heads with disgust. The second year, hardly anybody came except for the few families involved. The excitement, and thrill of Christmas that we knew as a church community was gone.

God had withdrawn His Spirit from the productions. And 'the so-called elites' were so pompous they never understood or cared what they did to the Church Community.

Except, God wasn't finished with me. I loved the Lord with all my heart and will to the day I go home to Him. Jim and I are firm believers in partaking the Eucharist as much as possible to sustain us. So, after we left OLOH, we picked up Jim's father Fred, who always attended Mass with us, and went to the Spanish Mass at the Basilica of St. Paul's Catholic Cathedral in Daytona Beach.

Looking back, I felt sorry for Jim and Fred. Neither of them spoke a word of Spanish. Fred was so understanding and helped ease my anxiety by telling me how proud he was of the productions. And that he appreciated me giving him the part of the voice of God, during CCD when Jesus was baptized by John the Baptist. He also added that years ago, the priest spoke only Latin during Mass with his back turned away from the congregation. It is the Eucharist that is important. He didn't care what language was spoken.

Chapter Seventeen

God Hears Our Prayers

God had another plan in mind for me, and in only a few months His plan of getting our family back into an English-Speaking Mass was clear. Remember what I said about God putting people in your path that either you need, or they need you?

About three months later, I met a new friend through one of Jim's acquaintances that he met through a patient's Energy Saving Company. Lindi happened to be the girlfriend of one of the employees, Andy, who had also invented an energy saving device for boiler rooms up north. Andy had a Fortune 500 company at one time. They had a long-distance relationship until Lindi moved to Daytona to be with Andy.

Interestingly enough, Lindi was Catholic most of her life, but for some reason started going to an Evangelical Church after her husband died. Her two children were grown, so she moved to Tampa for a much-needed change of scenery.

We had known each other for a few months when Lindi questioned me about why we attended a Spanish Mass when we didn't speak Spanish. She tried multiple times for Jim and me to attend her new Evangelical Church in South Daytona closer to our home. Finally, I explained the reason to her. Well, that struck a major nerve in Lindi, and she insisted we attend Our Lady of Hope (OLOH) together.

Since my devotion to the Trinity, Mother Mary, the Saints, and Angels is so strong, I was hoping to get Lindi back into the Catholic Faith. I learned first-hand that the politics in a church can be so crusty, but I would never turn away from my faith. After being the Pro-Life Chairman for the Orlando Diocese, I had spoken at all the Catholic Churches in the area and tried to steer her towards some near her apartment across the river, but to no avail. So, only in the interest of getting Lindi back to the Catholic Faith, I agreed to attend OLOH with her and Andy.

When Sunday came around, Jim took his car and picked up his father Fred. I drove my 'vette and parked in the back parking lot. We all met by the Parish Center and walked into the church together. I couldn't walk two feet without countless people coming up to greet me. When we got inside, the South Africa Priest was officiating the Mass. Even though he spoke several languages fluently, his heavy accent made his English hard to understand. I had heard through the grapevine that people wouldn't attend his Mass, because they couldn't understand what he was saying. Oddly enough, I could, especially since he rented an apartment from one of our neighbors and jogged daily in front of our house. Jim and I would run into him often and stop and talk to him.

After Mass, I wanted to go home but Lindi insisted we go into the Parish Center for coffee and donuts. I was barely inside the door when Fr. Ray, Deacon Mike Petitt, and the new pastor entered. I had heard through a friend that the Orlando Diocese had to bring Fr. Ray back, since attendance had drastically dropped after he retired.

The new pastor walked away, while Fr. Ray, and Deacon Mike gave me a hug welcoming me back. Many others came up to me with the same greeting. I noticed the pastor seemed to be carefully watching me from afar. I also noted that 'the self-proclaimed elites' snubbed me.

As Lindi and I were leaving the Parish Center, the new pastor grabbed the long bar that opens the glass door and held it shut. He said to me, "They say you're Kathe Hether." So, I was right about him watching me. It was startling to say the least. He could have easily stayed and talked with Fr. Ray, and the deacon instead of walking away. I wondered for a second what his angle was before I answered, "yes, I am."

Then he said something extremely disturbing while still holding the door shut, he asked me, "Why did you come back?"

I was shocked and speechless! I glanced at Lindi as she stared at him in disbelief. I quietly prayed to God for help, and then said, "because this is my friend Lindi, who just moved here from the Tampa area. She was looking for a Catholic Church near where she lives and decided to check out OLOH."

What I also didn't know but God did, was the pastor had recently come to OLOH from Tampa. He asked Lindi if she attended his church. She grinned as he named the church, answering him with a simple "no."

That's when I reached around him, opened the door, and we walked outside joining Andy, Jim, and Fred. To this very day, I wonder what 'the self-proclaimed elites' said about me causing his un-priestlike behavior. The Nineth Commandment is, "Thou shalt not bear false witness against thy neighbor."

God's Second Reason for That Day

As I was walking back to the 'vette, I heard 'the same voice' in my head that called me to do the productions, telling me 'to turn around, and tell the South African Priest that I liked his homily.' But, by this time, I was fuming about the new pastor's behavior! All the years of taking time off work, freely giving hours of my time and talent to further the work of Christ. All I wanted was to get off that property and go home! So, I kept walking.

God knew that I was hurt beyond words. As I continued to walk toward the 'vette. I heard the same request, 'turn around and tell the South African Priest, you liked his homily.' I couldn't believe he would still be standing in the same place, so I glanced over my shoulder. Sure enough, the South African Priest was still standing at the same spot in the parking lot by himself.

I heard it again a third time and obediently turned around, hurrying back to the South African Priest. I did as The Lord requested, telling him that I enjoyed his homily, and we talked for a few more minutes about being neighbors. He remembered that our big friendly dog, Capone, tried to jog with him once until we called him back.

What I didn't realize at that point, was God had an important reason for slowing me down. As I turned to walk back to the 'vette suddenly, a car I didn't recognize, sped into the parking lot driving directly towards me. The car almost hit me! I had to jump out of the way! I froze in my tracks wondering, 'what now?' The car pulled into a parking spot.

A very thin, frail lady slowly opened the car door, trying several times to stand up. I didn't recognize her at first, until she called my name, "Kathe." I couldn't believe my eyes, but voices never change. "Maggie, is that you?" I asked.

I rushed to Maggie's car, helping her get out, and hugged her. I hadn't seen her in two years and was in disbelief that her health had changed so drastically. She said, "I've had you on my mind ever since she named two women of the 'self-proclaimed elites,' who had flown up north to her home state for a weekend, out of the clear blue sky. They came to tell me that you quit the production. They wanted to know, if I would work with them on props.

I've been praying that I would get to see you before I leave tomorrow. I've been diagnosed with three kinds of cancers. One kind the doctor doesn't even know what it is. My son arrived yesterday to take me home to die. I've been praying that God would let me tell you goodbye."

We talked a while about the good times we had working on the productions together. She started to walk away, stopped, turned around, and said, "you know, after they took over, no one wanted to be in the plays, and no one wanted to come see the plays. All the years we enjoyed as a Church Community were gone, because of their greed. I knew they lied to me when they came to see me and told me that you didn't want to do them anymore. The Christmas Productions were the highlight of my coming back to Port Orange every year."

We hugged again and parted ways. I cried all the way home. A couple of weeks later, I attended a Memorial Service at OLOH for my Maggie. We weren't just a Church Community, God had clearly called a Church Family.

God Spared Maggie As A Newborn

One more glimpse of Maggie's incredible life that she shared with me was similar to Frank's encounter with Simeon. On one production, I asked Maggie if she could use all blue lights around the nativity scene. She immediately burst out into tears. I explained that I just wanted to change the nativity set to a night scene this year. That year's Christmas theme was Christmas Around the World. At the grand finale, a caravan of all the characters would be wearing their native clothing, carrying beautifully wrapped lit presents to give to the Holy Family.

137

After Maggie calmed down, she shared with me that her mother had always decorated their families Christmas Trees with lit candles on the tree. It was a German custom brought to America. Their house was located at the bottom of a hill. When Maggie was a newborn asleep in her crib, the house caught fire. Her mother got all her siblings outside, but her father couldn't get through the flames upstairs to the nursery for her. When the firemen arrived, they tried to get upstairs, but it was too dangerous. The firemen couldn't get a ladder near the nursery window, also due to the flames on the roof below. The Fire Chief finally ordered his men not to go back inside the house. Maggie's mother had a great faith in God. She began to pray with her husband and the other children for God to save Maggie.

All of a sudden, a fireman out of nowhere, appeared at the top of the hill. He ran down the hill past them, straight inside the house without slowing down. A few minutes later, he carried Maggie outside safely in his arms, handed her to her mother, ran straight back up the hill, and was gone. He never spoke a single word.

None of the other firemen knew who he was, since there were no markings on his suit, and he was never seen again. With his helmet covering his face, her mother didn't see what he looked like. From that moment on, they never had a Christmas Tree. Instead, her mother put a nativity scene inside the empty fireplace, lit with only blue lights. Maggie's mother always said that God sent an angel to save her life that night.

Now Maggie and Frank are both in heaven. I'll never forget the impact they've had on my life. As a side note at Christmastime, I can still feel the warmth of their smiles, along with the gleam in their eyes of excitement, and their hardy laughter of Christmas Joy. They are not gone, they just stepped out of our realm into God's realm with Him.

No one can ever take God's miracles away from us during those years. The gleam in the eyes, the smiles, the laughter's, the limelight, the memories that we all shared, will live on forever in the memories of the entire cast and crew.

Chapter Eighteen

God's Continued Guidance

Joshua 1:9 "Have I not commanded you? Be strong and courageous. Do not be terrified, do not be discouraged, for the Lord your God will be with you wherever you go." This scripture gave me such comfort as I continued to grow in faith, literary skills, and in the health field.

I turned my attention to working in Jim's Chiropractic Clinic as a Licensed Massage Therapist. When I look back, I can see the hand of God preparing me for a new path within the last few years that I did the productions. As busy as I was donating my time and talents to the church, Jim insisted that I also get a Massage Therapy License at the International Academy in South Daytona. It was very disruptive to patient's care when a therapist called in sick at the last minute. And canceling eight, one-hour massages cost the clinic quite a bite of money. As part owner of the clinics, it made sense, so I agreed. Plus, Jim promised that I would only work once in a while on an emergency basis.

God helped me with juggling my schedule to have quality time with my last teenage children living at home, housewife duties, script writing, play practices, and studying Anatomy and Physiology. Since I hadn't cracked open a college book in quite a few years, and my duties as a mother and wife never stopped, I found myself feeling overwhelmed as I started dinner after the first day of school.

Not to mention, I had a test the first thing in the morning. I remember going into the bedroom, getting on my knees, asking God for help. Instantly, I had a feeling that I should wake up every morning at 3:00 am to study. When I thought about it, that made a lot of sense. That is when everyone in the family would leave me alone, including a college daughter's Chihuahua, named Bruiser.

So, I began every morning for the next nine months at 3:00 am. I always began with a prayer asking for wisdom in understanding, and retaining the knowledge of a subject that really wasn't my passion in life. Again, I turned to James 1:5 "If anyone lacks wisdom, let him ask of God, who gives to all men generously without reproaching, and it will be given him." This scripture is not limited to studying and understanding the Bible. It proved to be a blueprint for any wisdom needed in life.

Also, sitting in Continued Education Seminars with Jim throughout our marriage paid off when I realized that I had retained most of the materials. As I began filling in for other therapists, patients began requesting me. With the Physical Therapy and X-ray Classes I sat through with Jim, I was way ahead of most of the other therapist.

Next, I could see God's hand gently encouraging me to learn other modalities to help patients. Isaiah 54:2 "Enlarge the site of your tent and let the curtains of your habitations be stretched out; do not hold back; lengthen your cords and strengthen your stakes." To me, this scripture isn't just about your house size, it means your knowledge.

After a surgical procedure, I was left with a large, thick scar around the lower half of my body. My skin felt tight across it, and when I laid in the sun on the beach, it burned. I had been praying for help to relieve the pain. That's when I received a flyer in the mail for CEU's at a Micro-Point Stimulation Course (MPS). The first day I attended class, I was hooked. It taught how to get rid of scar tissue, as well as heal many other ailments of the body.

That helped patients as well as me more than anything. I still use it today.

Looking back, God's guidance was with me as I studied and began clinical requirements at International Academy's Clinic. For the first time in the history of the academy, there was a waiting list for me in the clinic. One of the ladies at the front desk admitted that people would call, and book with me in advance for several weeks at a time. They had to put a limit on the number of visits per person. There was a waiting list of other people refusing to see the other students. Instead, they insisted on waiting until I could see them.

What was my secret to success in clinical work? As I began each massage with the patient face down under the sheets, I would put both my hands on the patient's back, say a quick, silent prayer asking for God's guidance to help with their particular problem. I always ended with a light, small Sign of the Cross on their back. To my surprise, I had several patients ask me to pray with them throughout the years, which was very humbling.

Jim began using me more on a regular basis, which I never planned or wanted to do. His patients began asking solely for me. However, it wasn't until I met two, special people at the office when I realized why God had a reason for my 'healing hands.' God wanted me to pursue my passion in a writing career.

That's where I began having "Forever Friendships" that God brought into my life for specific reasons. The first was Jean Tessier. She was single and worked for the government. Her family lived in Kentucky and other parts of the country. On the weekends, she was an avid movie watcher. She would ask me what movies I liked during our sessions. I remember telling her that I didn't watch too many movies, because I was too busy writing and directing musical productions for my church.

After she attended that year's Christmas Productions, she asked me if I had written anything else. I told her that since I had so many children, and didn't have time to volunteer in their classrooms, I would write children's stories and read them in class. And I had a manuscript for a book that I wrote back in the eighties, hoping someday it would be used in a movie.

Long story short, I loaned Jean the large manuscript (540-pages) on a Friday afternoon after her appointment. On Monday afternoon, she came back with the manuscript. She read the entire thing over the weekend, and told me that she couldn't put it down. All the fictitious, scientific technology that I imagined within the manuscript back in the early eighties existed today.

One example of this is the main character, Kathe Tierny used a small cell phone that hung from her belt that she called (JAKE) to talk with Alby Airline's Control, which also was computerized to answer her questions. Cell phones had just come out in the eighties. Most of them were either part of the car's console or they were as big as a backpack. They were only used to call people in emergency situations, due to the high cost of using them. They also weren't able to converse with humans. The fact is, they were plain large phones.

Today everyone has a cell phone with (Siri) which is part of AI to answer questions. Also, Tierney had an implant under her right, clavicle that control could locate her at a moment's notice, which is GPS. That was not invented yet. Jean told me that I needed to upgrade the technology and then publish it. And that was the beginning of our 'Forever Friendship.'

While Jean was daily helping me revamp the manuscript after work, on the weekends since she lived 30 miles away, she'd stay at our house. That way we had more time to work together. We always began every session with prayer. That was when I found out that she was Catholic. During those years, Jean attended three years of the Christmas Productions. She couldn't believe how very diverse the shows were from the Romance/Mystery that she was helping me update. She was impressed that not too many writers could switch genre that easily.

Even now with us living in different states, we're still the best of friends. We've spent hours upon hours bouncing ideas off each other over the phone. My characters in the Project Series are imbedded in her brain like mine. Many times, after reworking a scene during the daytime, she would email me in the wee hours of the morning because she couldn't sleep due to an idea popping into her head. Since the main character was a flight attendant, if we had a question concerning the duties, she would call her sister Anne, who at that time worked for Southwest Airlines.

That is one reason the characters in my novels are so strong. One thing I learned is that people like to talk about themselves. While working on patients from different professions, they would explain their particular duties. I've had the privilege of working on Artists, Nurses, Doctors, School Teachers, Musicians, Flight Attendants, Airline Pilots, Vietnam Huey (Helicopter) Pilots, EMT's, Firemen, Police Officers, Highway Patrolmen, Small Business Owners, TSA Officers, Weapon's Experts, Underwater Explosive Experts, Underwater Treasure Hunters, Government Employees, and many more. Each person gave me such inspiration learning about their line of work, it enhanced the strength of my characters.

The first manuscript I was inspired to write in the early eighties, Project Chameleon/XP 38, I wrote with the intent of becoming a movie. I can remember going to the now non-existent Blockbuster Movie Rentals. I could almost feel myself reaching for a copy of the movie. Jean noticed I accomplished this from the first page she read of the manuscript. She said many times that with the visual way I write, it was like watching a movie. She was also the first person who believed in me and urged me to keep the series going.

The Second Person God Sent To Me

As you well know by now, I've always been a firm believer that 'Coincidence is God's way of staying anonymous.' And, when I least expected it,' is another one of 'God's Miracle Moments' happening in my life.

So, 'when I least expected it', God sent Filmmaker, Stephen Brown into my life in an unimaginable way. I would soon find out that Steve has an incredible belief in God. As our friendship grew, we became prayer partners for both our families and friends with problems.

When Steve first came into our office, he was working in Clearwater, Florida, which was about four hours away from Daytona filming the famous, Baby Dolphin, Winter with the prosthetic tailfin, at the Clearwater Marine Aquarium (CMA).

The news of Winter's fate of not expecting to live through that first night, to surviving the amputation, touched the heart of Kevin Carroll, Vice President of Prosthetics at the Hanger Clinic. He designed and made Winter's new tailfin. Steve filmed Kevin attaching the prosthetic tale for the first time, and Winter swimming around with it.

145

It was Steve's passion filming all hours of the day and night, documenting Winter's tenacity learning to use her one-of-a-kind prosthetic tailfin. It was through the lens of Steve's camera that brought people with disabilities from adults to children around the world to see 'Winter The Dolphin That Could.'

That is the name of one of Steve's documentaries on Winter. As Steve continued filming Winter, he said her story reminded him of a ballad. He contacted a musical friend of his, Pastor Pete, asking him to write a ballad for the documentary, 'The Ballad of Winter' became the theme song, and Steve sang harmony with the pastor when they recorded it. In his modesty, Steve forgot to mention that he has an incredible singing voice.

Again, as Steve would tell me his story about Winter, to this writer, it clearly showed me that 'Coincidence is God's way of staying anonymous'. It was Winter's destiny all along that God had planned for her to be an 'earthly angel' and inspiration to thousands. That's how she was able to live sixteen years in captivity after her accident as a small calf.

As you have come to know, I believe in angels, some heavenly and some earthly. Winter's life and even after her death on November 11, 2021, is still God's inspiration to many with disabilities ranging from adults, combat, military men and women, veterans, teenagers to small children that were either born or injured and now living with disabilities. However, as quick as Steve came into our office, he healed and was gone.

God's Plan For Us Continued

About six months later, Steve came back to my office after a horrific knee injury while still filming at CMA. He told me that the first time he saw me, I was able to get him back to work

146

in such a short time using MPS, that while recovering from knee surgery this time, he requested me to do his therapy.

I'll never forget the day that Steve insisted on reading my manuscript on a Wednesday morning. Jokingly, he laughed and said, "I better read it, or God will make sure I need your services again until I do." With Steve being a devout Christian, and a filmmaker, that gave me hope that God sent him to help me, which he did.

This proved to be the beginning of a second 'Forever Friendship' between us. Steve admitted when he came back a second time that he remembered I was writing a novel. On Friday, Steve asked me if I brought the manuscript. When I showed it to him, he refused to leave until I signed it. And at that time, he let me borrow the only copy he had of a documentary he just finished, 'Winter The Dolphin That Could' featuring the song, 'Ballard of Winter.' © 2009

Steve also read the 540-page manuscript over the weekend. Monday morning at 8:00 am, he was raving about the each of the characters, the storyline, and the potential for a Hollywood Movie or TV Series, that could run for years with a female version of a James Bond movie.

Steve said that no matter what page the reader started on, one could easily follow the storyline. He too said it was like watching a movie. He particularly like the fact that I never used foul language or sex scenes in the Romance/Mystery Novel, even with the main Christian Character accidently getting pregnant. He said the scene happened and was over before he realized it. That made it suitable for audiences ranging from young teenagers to adults.

Steve's company, Gabby Mobile Productions produced the covers of all three so-far of the Project Series. It was so awesome watching Steve take my storyline and through his eyes create the covers to market them.

Steve also initiated a think-tank with Jean, Jim, and I throwing around ideas for the next two novels. During one of our sessions, we learned that Steve was in the Special Forces. He was sent into the jungles of Vietnam to gather information for the government, before our troops were sent to fight in the war. At age eighteen in 1967, Jim was sent to Vietnam to fight in that war, where he was badly injured. From that moment, the two of them had a special bond.

Steve was always inventing different ways to stay ahead of the film industry. He incorporated drones into my novels, since he helped design cameras for a high-tech drone, each carrying 12, 360-degree cameras with 8K resolution to film documentaries. With permission I made characters of Steve and his employees and put them into the storyline.

The scene in Project Wraith, where Steve's character calls Dr. Sydney about using his drone over Haul Over Canal (page 295) filming rare birds along with someone from the Audubon Society. As the story continues, he and his crew were filming when a helicopter marked Homeland Security, shot his drone out of the sky, even though it was clearly marked and he is licensed to use it. Luckily, he was live streaming it to his studio. He didn't realize until they went to his studio that the drone also caught on camera a boat with a man unconscious lying on the bottom between the seats. The unconscious man was Yorg in the book that the mob had just kidnapped. That marked the beginning of my using drones in the rest of the two books, and it will be used in the books to follow.

In Project Canaveral, Steve's character again has a prominent role getting Kathe Tierney's Team into Cuba with his

148

film company. It is his use of drones that helps locate and neutralize the enemies. Again, his knowledge of drones and travel experience are what brings the realism to life in the storyline.

Since Steve is just a little older than Jim and me with only one granddaughter, he was always amazed at how I was able to juggle my busy schedule with work and a very large family to include time to write. What I learned about Steve, was that he lived a very exciting life traveling the world while filming famous people and places. I remember telling him once that he lived the kind of life I'd always dreamt of having. That's when he admitted that kind of lifestyle isn't what it's chalked up to be. Then, he shared with Jim and I that he had walked away from God for a while.

There was a song back in the 60's, 'Smuggler's Blues' that was written about Steve's life prior to finding Christ. But once Steve found Christ, he never let go! He told me that from that moment on, he begins every morning with reading the scriptures. Taking time with God brings Him with you throughout the day.

It was Steve's constant faith in seeing God in everything he did, that inspired me to write 'A Gift of His Mercy.' I wanted to give Steve a unique Christmas gift that he could read every Christmas to his granddaughter. A story that would take them on an incredible journey of faith together. With permission I used Steve and Joanna's names in the story for them to enjoy reading year after year. To this day at Christmastime, they read 'A Gift of His Mercy' and still love it.

'A Glimpse of His Life' is the second of a series that take Steve and Joanna on another journey. This time they go back into the Biblical Scriptures to witness the birth, life, death, and resurrection of our Lord and Savior for the Lenten and Easter Season.

Isn't it just like God to put two people together that have absolutely nothing in common, only to find out that they have everything in common through Christ. It is this shared faith in Christ that cements 'Forever Friends' together forever. Plus, God recently blessed Steve after living many years alone with a wonderful, talented, Christian wife, Darlene.

Through Christ Families Strengthen In Crisis Situations

This brings me to my third and fourth 'Forever Friends' who are my identical, twin sister-in-law's Jane Self and Jeanie Borden. They are two special Christians who also put God first in their lives. They share the same thirst for studying the scriptures as I do. They also understand the concept in using them, as God's blueprint to handle life's ups and downs.

As I wrote in Chapter One, being a Christian parent of a large family didn't give me a free pass from problems. This holds true with Jeanie and Jane's families and they each only had two children. The size of a family doesn't make the heartaches less painful. With Christ joining us in prayer, we got through the most, difficult times together. Matthew 18:20 "For where two or three are gathered in My Name, there am I in the midst of them."

At one time, Jim and I had two, teenage daughters that seemed to be double-teaming us at the same time with separate, major issues. I remember kneeling by my bedside day after day, crying unto the Lord for help with daughters out- of-control. I even called Father Lopez High School in Daytona and asked if they could take my two daughters from Hades and turn them into debutants. But to no avail. They didn't take troubled teenagers.

It got so bad, that the girls problems started consuming every moment of my life. I couldn't remember the last time I laughed. It was so bad at play practice, even the actors noticed it. I'll never forget that during an Adam and Eve scene, Eve was reaching for the apple. Adam jumped out wearing a flesh-colored leotard complete with a cape and mask saying, "I'll save you Eve! Don't touch that apple! You'll destroy mankind, and Kathe will never laugh again!"

I didn't know whether to laugh or cry. I could feel everybody's eyes staring at me. I finally broke out into hardy laughter. That's when I realized there are some things in life, you can't handle alone.

At least, Jim had a break going to work five days a week. I was the one the school or police would call. It wasn't long after that play practice when I received a phone call that was the straw that broke the camel's back-my back. Kneeling, I prayed through tears for God to see and feel my pain. I explained that I had developed splinters on my knees from frequently requesting help, without receiving any response. I couldn't stand another day of this and there was no mansion in heaven worth this constant drama. It was affecting the other children as well.

Since my bedroom floor was carpeted, that bold prayer got God's attention, and He did send me help. I would be lying to you, if I didn't tell you that it wasn't exactly the answer that I was looking for. But I would soon learn that God answered my prayer with His even bolder answer. God's answer was that drugs were involved.

Being a Chiropractic family, we never had a medicine cabinet in the bathroom. We had a toothpaste cabinet. From early on, we taught the children that drugs were bad, pushed or prescribed. The earlier you get hooked on them, that's when your

151

brain stops growing. Look around you in this generation today. Older drug addicts act, talk, and behave still like young teenagers.

After all the faith and witnessing about the Lord I have written about, suddenly I was thrown into a deep valley that I didn't see coming. A crisis that hit me in the face like 'Job' must have felt. That's when I turned to the scriptures. Hebrew 10:24,25 seemed to jump out at me. "And let us consider how to stir up one another to love and good works, not neglecting to meet together, as in the habit of some, but encouraging one another, and all the more as you see The Day drawing nearby." The Day the scriptures refers to is in the last day before Christ returns. Well to me and Jim, The Day had come!

Around that time Jane's husband, Wayne had just been diagnosed with cancer. That's when Jim and I learned a very, valuable lesson; one that has stayed with me to this day. Wayne was a prominent Christian Businessman in Daytona, who along with several ministers and friends, started Stewart Marchman Rehab Center for Drug and Alcohol Abuse.

I'll never forget the question Wayne asked us as we conversed about our out-of-control daughters. Even though he wasn't a counselor, as a Christian and a father, he answered Jim and I in sort of a parable like Jesus taught. He said, "Imagine praying to God for help, and suddenly finding yourself in a room full of similar devastated people, sitting in a circle. Within that circle each person was asked to tell their problems and then place them in the center of the circle. After the last person spoke, we were then told that we could change problems by choosing from the circle or take our own problems home." Then, Wayne asked, "After we finished listening to everyone's problems, would we pick our own problems and go home? Or would we pick the problem of a couple who just lost a child to drug overdose, or

152

a family facing bankruptcy, or Wayne's problem of being diagnosed with cancer? Which problem would we take home?" At that moment, our problems seemed so trivial. We chose to take our own problem home standing in faith that God would help us.

Even with all the miracles Jim and I have witnessed in our lives, after a while of being bombarded with one crisis after another, life wears you down. It happens to everyone sooner or later. Wayne's mini parable reminded us to stand steadfast in faith. Isaiah 26:3 "You will keep in perfect peace him whose mind is steadfast because he trusts in The Lord."

God showed us what the problem was that the girls were facing. Wayne helped us get them the help they needed. He sent a referral to Stewart Marchman for the girls to start treatment.

It is this unique special bond with Christ, that we as a family shared, which would soon hold the Hether Family together when faced with several tragedies, that seemed like a long line of tumbling dominoes. It affected the entire Hether Family, but Jim's sister Jeanie would be put through the 'Refiner's Fire', since it affected her immediate family.

In a relatively, short span of time of about six months, Jeanie would see the death of her first husband, Murphy, her older brother, Fred, her identical, twin, sister Jane, would have a heart attack and be brought back to life. Jeanie would assist Jane's daughters to help Jane relearn life's daily chores and bring her memory back. Jeanie's husband, Bill was suddenly diagnosed with an aggressive cancer and quickly passed away. Jeanie and Jane decided to go on a vacation with church friends to Nova Scotia as a get-a-way. While on the vacation, Jane decided to run up a steep mountain to get a picture of an old church. She tripped and fell, striking her head, taken to a hospital that had socialized

153

medicine. With the lack of proper care, Jane passed away. Then, not long after Jeanie got home, her youngest daughter passed away. Not long after this, one of her and Bill's dogs died, and she had to bury him in the backyard.

Jeanie became a 'Pillar of Strength' to all those around her. She saw God's hand in every aspect of her life. She said that each time a tragedy struck, God always sent someone immediately to be with her, even in Nova Scotia. Instead of letting her grief consume her, she decided to get out of the house three or four times a day. She volunteered at Our Lady of Hope's Thrift Store near her house. She also volunteered at her own church by baking cakes to sell at the church's café and joined a widow's group to help comfort and strengthen them.

Even with Jeanie's busy schedule, her large house was empty, so another widow, Sandy from her church moved in with her. They both stay busy helping others in need. Last Christmas, when Daytona still had houses flooded from the hurricanes, God sent those two ladies along with some of their friends on a mission to deliver twenty decorated Christmas Trees with presents to the needy in the area. People seem to come out of nowhere with extra trees, ornaments, and gifts to donate to their cause. It was such an outpouring of love, they ended up with thirty, fully decorated trees along with gifts.

The stories of God leading them to people in need are amazing. One woman answered the door and saw a blessing from God. She broke into tears when she saw what they had. Christmas was coming up, and she didn't have a tree or presents for her small children. She also was missing her mother, and her children didn't get to know a grandmother's love. So, God sent five grandmothers to deliver the trees.

And it all started with Sandy and her belief in God. She doesn't know the words, 'can't do'. She only knows 'with God all things are possible.' Lamentations 3:25 "The Lord is good to those whose hope is in Him, to the ones who seek Him."

Isn't that what God meant when He said the greatest commandment is love? 'Forever Friends' are just that. You know, the ones you can call day or night when you need strength. It is a blessing to have Jean, Jeanie, Sandy, Jim, Darlene, and Steve as part of my Florida Prayer Group. In Utah, where we live now, I have our Bible Study Group, and I'm a member of the St. John the Baptist Catholic Church's Prayer Warriors for a second support team when sickness, stress and anxiety rear its ugly head.

Chapter Nineteen

A Move Blessed by God

It's strange how God closes one door and opens another door in our lives. Some of our adult children were aging us terribly with their problems. They didn't listen to us when we tried to help them. Jim and I cried out to God with contrite hearts to help us, and He did.

Jim had been trying to sell an apartment building for years with no luck. To make things worse, we signed a 'Personal Guarantee' with the bank and our house was collateral. The apartment building was in a part of town, which some of the tenants made a living off the system by not paying rent. They knew exactly how long it would take for Jim to file a complaint of non-payment with the courts, then he would get a three-day notice for their door, then a seven-day notice, and then how long they had before the Sherriff posted the eviction notice on their door. Basically, how long they could live rent-free off us. Of course, our mortgage and insurance companies needed their money on time, no matter what.

Honestly, we looked around, and even though we finally had our house just like we wanted, the pros and cons of Florida compared to Utah's mountains were sizable. So, we thought about putting our house on the market. We visited Utah again, decided that's where we wanted to live, came home, and put our home on the market.

We buried a statue of St. Joseph upside down by our front door and then placed another one at the apartment building. Almost a year went by with no luck on either place.

We took another trip to Utah, found the perfect house on top of a mountain with an incredible view of Utah Valley below us.

We came home and began boldly praying to God to help us move. We put large pictures of the mountain home in front of the television in the family room, concepting that house. That's when we sold our house and the apartment building on the same day and in the same hour. We were blessed by God selling both at once to two different people. It was a miracle! But not a big enough miracle for the Lord to show us how great He is.

We flew to Utah and put a contract on the mountain home contingent on our Florida house closing in one month. Our Utah relator warned us a week later that the sellers had remorse and didn't want to sell the house. Bottom line, the only thing keeping the sale legal was holding them to our contract.

A week before the movers were to be at our Florida home, I went to get my nails done. Jim was busy last-minute packing in the garage when he received a phone call. The contract on our Florida home fell through six days before our contract agreement in Utah had to be fulfilled to be legal. When I got home, Jim gave me the bad news.

Devastated, Jim and I got on our knees boldly praying to God to give us a new buyer immediately. The apartment building sold a week earlier. But we couldn't move without the money from the sale of our house.

By law, we had to tell our Utah relator the contract fell through. The sellers that had remorse instantly moved back into the house. When I heard that I ran into our bedroom, got on my knees again, and with tears in my eyes cried out in prayer to the Lord. All of a sudden, God reminded me that there was another couple who wanted the house. I called our Florida relator, and he remembered the people and called them.

Those people had a contract on another home but liked ours more. So, they came by the next morning for another look to decide. God had arranged for another miracle because in two days legally was the last day they could back out of that contract. By the grace of God, it all worked out and they bought our home!

But that's not all, at that point our contract date fell on a weekend. We thought we had until Monday to close. However, our Utah relator on Wednesday said in order to keep the original contract, we had to close by Friday. Utah law read if the closing date falls on a weekend, the closing went back to Friday. In the State of Florida when a contract ends on a weekend it carries over to Monday.

When our Florida relator called the new buyers, they miraculously were able to pay cash for the house. Which meant, we were able to close in two days on Friday. God truly had us in the palm of His hands.

Two More Miracles Back-to-Back

Seven years later, living in our beautiful, mountain home, one of the two air-conditioners broke. It just so happened that two days before, we had just switched our home warranty company. With the terrible inflation in America's economy that the Biden Administration caused, our income was stretched thin. This was difficult with both of us retired, and Jim a Disabled Veteran. Jim was panicking over money to cover our deductible. He was also worried that since we just changed companies, would they cover our air conditioner.

158

If that wasn't enough, we were standing outside on our deck at the time, noticing that several of our neighbors were getting new roofs. Jim reminded me that our roof was now over twenty-five years old. The weather here is pretty destructive with the snow and high winds during the winter, and the scorching heat in the desert's summer.

I will never forget what I told Jim. "I don't know how we're going to get the money, but I do know we have faith in God. When we least expect it, God will give us the money."

Jim called the new home warranty company on Monday morning. They approved the claim, and the air-conditioner cost us $1,500.00. That covered our deductible and the price of a new air-handler. Our original air-handler was so old, it wasn't compatible with the new technology of the new one.

But that's not all God heard that day. The Lord heard the same faith I had in Him standing on the altar at Our Lady of Hope Catholic Church, while talking with Leanne several years earlier. I used the term, 'when we least expect it, God will find us a Baby Jesus.' And as you read in one of the earlier chapters, God lead me out of town to meet a family with a newborn baby, plus two older brothers to be the sheep we needed.

Having that same faith in God proved right again. When Jim and I least expected it, in the middle of June out of the blue, a tremendous hailstorm hit our neighborhood, destroying our roof. Our Homeowner's Insurance covered $29,000.00 out of the $30,000.00 price of the roof. We had to pay the $1,000.00 deductible. 1 John 5:15-16 is the blueprint in the Bible that reveals this kind of faith. "And this is the confidence we have in Him, that if we ask anything according to His will, He hears us, and if we know that He hears us in whatever we ask, we know that we have obtained the request made of Him."

God's Abundance of Miracles

When I mentioned several of our neighbors needed new roofs, I remembered another grace God granted us. When we bought our house one of our six, large, view windows overlooking the valley below us leaked. It was still under warranty, and we had it replaced.

Two years ago, after a winter of constant snowfall, followed by intense rain with high winds during the springtime, some of our immediate neighbors had flooding. The window we replaced in our living room leaked down into the first floor through the walls. We had never seen anything like it. Our insurance wouldn't cover it, since it was an Act of God. Some of our neighbors found black mold inside their walls as a result of the intense constant storms. The out-of-pocket cost was extremely high.

It was also the spring Jim and I decided to move back to Florida. Jim re-herniated his L4-L5 vertebrae from his injuries in Vietnam, because of the constant snowplowing. As we were trying to sell our house, one of the downstairs windows leaked horribly. If that wasn't bad enough, I ended up for the first time allergic to petunias and lilies causing asthma and difficulty in breathing. This caused me to panic and shot my blood pressure sky high. The hospital gave me a medicine to bring my blood pressure down, which immediately caused an adverse, allergic reaction, causing me to go into Atrial Fibrillation. Even after all this, Jim and I stayed in faith.

Again, living off retirement under the Biden Administration had our finances in disarray. We had to come up with the money to replace the window, which this time was not under warranty.

Jim and I stood in front of the window using Holy Water, we boldly asked Jesus to help us replace the window, and that there would be NO mold in the walls. And the Lord already had that covered for us.

A window company the next day left a flyer on our door. Jim called them and we had a year and a half with no interest to pay for the windows. The price included replacing six windows. When the workers replaced the leaky window, the wood under it was rotten with absolutely NO mold anywhere! We couldn't stop thanking Jesus for another one of His big miracles.

Looking back with all the problems we went through at the time, we said if God didn't want us to move, all He had to do was put a note in our mailbox. I never wanted to move to Florida and leave Paris, our granddaughter and her husband Skyler. I like living in the mountains. Plus, the reason we moved in the first place hadn't changed. Jim only wanted to get out of the snow and have a swimming pool that helped his low back issues.

Since living in Utah every time we visited Florida, we couldn't wait to get back to the mountains. Plus, Paris was having a hard time getting pregnant. I used Micro Point Stimulation (MPS) on her acupuncture points like I did several times to women with the same problem, and she got pregnant within two months. She and Skyler have a beautiful, baby boy, Ellis.

I hope by reading this book, you will understand the importance of taking time to think about all the things God has done throughout your life. Then, share the goodness of God to others, and they will do the same.

Our Blessings Multiplied

As I wrote this book, I shared some of my treasured moments with Christ with my daughter, Melody. We have consistently shared our experiences of divine blessings throughout our lives. As a young girl, she also witnessed the angel at our front door in Georgia and recalls the event clearly.

Last January, Melody's husband, John, passed away at age fifty-six due to kidney disease. She has always had a strong faith in God, as well as her four sons, which she proudly put through St. John Vianney High School in New Jersey. These are two of her most recent stories with Christ, that she shared with me.

A few days after Jim and I returned to Utah from the funeral, Melody called me one afternoon excited to tell me, "Mom, I just left someone that reminded me of you. She was older than dirt." And I interrupted, "Well, thanks for the compliment." Then, she said, "I didn't mean it like that. She reminded me of you and your faith."

Melody continued, "I went to the Post Office by my house in Brick after hours to mail my hand written thank you cards to people who came to John's funeral. Even though it had already closed, I knew the lobby was open, so I took my time putting stamps on the cards to drop in the mail slot. As I was busy putting the stamps on the cards, an elderly woman entered. I looked up for just a minute, and she gave me eye

162

contact. You don't understand Mom, in New Jersey and New York nobody gives eye contact to people they don't know."

Then, the woman loudly sighed, "Oh, no, they are closed too!" I walked over to her, asking if she needed help, and told her she could use the machine in the lobby for stamps. Then, she could drop it in the box like I was doing and offered her a stamp. She said, "No that's okay, I have a stamp, the only thing I wanted to do is to mail my important letter."

I quickly showed her where to put the letter in the mail slot as I did and said it would be picked up in the morning. I thought that was the end and started walking out into the parking lot. She was right behind me and thanked me for helping her, so I turned around and said, "you're welcome."

She responded, "No, you don't understand, you see I'm from Toms River (two towns away) and my Post Office was closed, so I was heading to the Barnegat Post Office (further down south in the opposite direction), and somehow my car brought me to Brick Post Office, which I hadn't been to in thirty years." She continued, "I have a special message for you, Jesus wanted me to tell you that everything will be alright and He's proud of you."

With that, I broke down into tears, right there in the parking lot. She grabbed me and gave me a big hug. I told her that I just lost my husband of thirty-three-years a week earlier. I felt so comfortable with her, that I also shared that I've been worried over the last six months about losing my job. My company was sending my entire division to Ireland. The woman smiled and said again, "God is proud of you, and everything is going to be fine." We shared one last hug, then parted ways.

Melody said to me, that woman must have been an angel that God sent to her when she needed it. Not long after that, she found out that her company decided to retain a few people, and she was one of them.

What I didn't share with Melody, was the angel's message was the exact wording of several of my Rosaries over the last six months, that I prayed for her and the boys. I boldly reminded God that I know Melody has a fantastic Guardian Angel. But I asked Him to please send a special, Messenger Angel to tell Melody that everything would be okay, and she would be able to keep her job. Jim and I are very proud of Melody, listening to how she was balancing taking care of John, helping the boys cope with his illness, and worrying about losing her income. Melody has been with the company for over twenty-six-years. It was clear, that this was truly a Messenger Angel sent from God to help my daughter, and her children.

After reading these witnesses of God, now more than ever, you should take a few minutes each week to jot down God's presence in your life. Read it often and watch your list grow like mine continues.

The next and last chapter goes into more details of my 'bout with asthma, and the scriptures I read daily of how God saved my life, like He has others by our faith in Him.

Chapter Twenty

Biblical Blueprint For Healing

In the summer of 2023, Jim and I came down with a virus which lasted six weeks, while taking care of four, small grandchildren. The Emergency Room doctor told me that the virus is so new it doesn't have a name; and that it only affects young children and the elderly.

Then as quickly as it came, almost overnight it was gone. For another month we were fine. We decided to move back to Florida, after experiencing the worst winter Utah had in the past eighty years.

An expert for our realtor came to show us what to do to stage the house for marketing. Properties were currently selling within six weeks or less after listing, often at above asking price due to the increase demand from individuals relocating from blue (democratic) states, especially California.

The news was warning that this inflation bubble was going to burst at any time. Our relator said only a few houses in Suncrest on top of Traverse Ridge Mountain were still available, that we had a week to get it ready for show.

This was extremely stressful for both of us. Especially, after just recovering from the 'no-name' virus. The designer suggested we use plug-in scents on each floor, since we have a dog.

We never used plug-in scents before due to the unhealthy chemicals in them. But we figured we should use them this time, only when showing the house.

After acquiring the recommended brand, I noticed that the fragrances consistently bothered me during each house showing. The issue escalated to the point where Jim had to remove them before I re-entered the house.

The last time we showed the house, I couldn't come inside until he put them in a Ziplock baggie, threw them in the garbage, and aired the house out. We even tried different scents, but those had the same effect on me.

After the snow finally melted, our grass was green, and our trees were budding. Our relator suggested that we buy black mulch for the large flower garden in the backyard and some flowers for the deck.

On Saturday afternoon, we went to Home Depot with the intent to try one more time to find a scent that didn't bother me. But as soon as I got on the soap/scent isle, I had to flee the store and use my inhaler. On the way home with petunias and mulch in the car, we had to roll the windows down for the same reason.

It was almost 4:30 pm by the time we got home. We decided to go to 5:00 pm Mass, so we could work on the house all day Sunday when Paris and Skyler could help us.

After Mass, we came home and sat with our dog, Sophie on the back porch near the petunias. I realized that even though we had petunias on our deck for the past three years, suddenly I was allergic to them. It got so bad; I ended up in the Emergency Room.

Long story short, my blood pressure went sky-high, because I couldn't breathe and panicked. The ER Doctor called St. Mark's Hospital to consult with a cardiologist about what to do for me, since everything they tried didn't work. He prescribed Hydralazine to bring the pressure down to keep me from having a stroke.

I immediately went into A-Fib for the first time. My blood pressure immediately dropped. However, my heartbeat raised and became very erratic. To save my life, they did a cardio version. Which means they used electric shock to stop my heart and slowly bring me back to life, putting my heart back into sinus rhythm.

I remember being so scared as they were getting me ready for the procedure. They glued electrical pads over my heart and on my upper back to conduct the electricity. Jim was standing inside the door watching them in fear.

Suddenly, as they got ready to start the procedure, a great calm came over me remembering that I had just taken the Eucharist. I was in total peace knowing I could wake up with Christ. I know without a shadow of doubt that it was my confidence in God that saved my life. It happened so fast I didn't realize it was over.

Afterwards, Jim said it was just like watching a scene in the movies. I raised off the table as the heart monitor flat lined. Then, slowly they used the same machine to restart my heart. By the grace of God, my heart was back in normal, sinus rhythm. A few minutes later, they unhooked the monitors and pads. I was taken back to my room where I got dressed and they released me.

The doctor changed the type of my inhaler, since I still had a hard time breathing and sent me home in the wee hours of the morning. The inhaler bothered my throat, and I developed a terrible scratchy throat and constant, hacking cough.

Our next-door neighbor heard about my ordeal. She brought dinner, and flowers for me. Jim put the flowers by my bedside as I slept. Later, when I woke up, I noticed I couldn't breathe again. I used the new inhaler, which didn't work. Jim checked my heart, and I was in A-fib again. He forgot that I was allergic to lilies. I went back to the same hospital.

A different ER Doctor was on shift, and I told her that it all began with plug-in scents and petunias. I also explained that asthma ran in my family. But the only way to treat A-fib was with cardio version, so I went through that again.

A month later, I had another cardio version caused by panicking due to not being able to breathe again. This time the ER Doctor kept me on an inhaler and added a nebulizer with steroids. I was to stagger them as needed. Even with the moisture in the nebulizer, nothing helped the scratchy throat and cough.

As the days went on, I ended up needing to use both treatments more often than prescribed. To be honest, by this time no one was helping me, and I didn't want to keep this up. By this time, I couldn't ride down the mountain without using my inhaler on the way back up to breathe. Once inside the house, I had to immediately use the nebulizer.

My oldest daughter, Melody, one of her sons, Johnny along with his girlfriend, Gia came to visit from New Jersey for a few days. It lifted my spirits, and we had fun, but I couldn't do much physically. Within a few months, I had gone from a happy, busy, outgoing person, to practically an invalid.

After they left, I was giving up hope that I would heal from this illness. I felt sorry for Jim; he hadn't had a good night sleep in months. He never complained and was always by my side. I'll never forget the night Jim got on his knees, hugging me as he cried begging God not to take his wife.

That night is when God saw the love in Jim's heart and gave us a miracle. I woke up needing a breathing treatment

168

about 3:00 am. While I was using the nebulizer, Jim turned on the television to stay awake. Our dog, Sophie curled up on the couch next to me.

God had set into motion a series of events to get me the help I needed. First, the TV turned on to the TBN Channel. We weren't watching that channel when we went to bed. There was no reason for the television to change stations. Secondly, it so happened, that Joel Osteen was giving a homily, which I had heard several times previously. When he was in college, his mother was diagnosed with liver cancer. There was nothing the doctors could do for her. They estimated that she had two weeks to live and sent her home. The camera switched to the front row, right in front of the podium, showing his mother sitting next to his wife, Victoria, and their two children.

His words were, 'Thirty-nine years later, Dodie Osteen is very much alive and well.'

This time Joel's sermon really caught my attention. How did Dodie Osteen overcome this death sentence? Jim and I eagerly watched the entire show, hanging on every word. Joel explained what Dodie did to heal her body. With Dodie, it didn't happen overnight. She had to let go of all the negative emotions that filled her thoughts. To do this, she began watching funny shows. Laughter is very healing. Proverbs 17:22 "A cheerful heart is good medicine, but a crushed spirit dries up the bones."

Next, she looked up all the healing scripture verses in the Bible and read them several times a day. Jim and I realized that Dodie was reprogramming her brain. Joel 3:10 "Let the week say, 'I am strong.'" Joel mentioned that to this day she reads them before leaving her house.

Finally, he shared exactly what I was looking for. Dodie had recently published a small book about her healing, including the scriptures she reads, and that she reads them on her YouTube Channel. Jim immediately pulled up Amazon and ordered the book.

We turned on YouTube and watched Dodie read her healing scriptures. My spirituality was not only charged, but on fire! At that moment, The Holy Spirit put into my mind to pray asking God to lead me to the right doctor. Jim and I held our left hands together, as we held up our right hands toward heaven and prayed. The word pulmonologist immediately came to me-loud and clear. A few hours later, as soon as the Cardiologist Department at St. Mark's Hospital opened, I called to get a referral.

What God already knew, and I didn't was the pulmonologist and my cardiologist worked in the same office, complete with the same front desk personnel. At first, there was no openings until late the next week. But an hour later, miraculously the office called back and there was a cancellation for tomorrow morning. Coincidence is God's way of staying anonymous.

The next morning at 8:00 am, I saw Stephanie Lowder, PA. at St. Mark's Hospital in Salt Lake City. She diagnosed me with acute asthma, brought on by sudden allergies to chemical scents, petunias, and lilies. She put me on Trelegy, a new inhaler and had me use it before I left her office.

Instantly, I could breathe better, and my coughing stopped. For the first time in a long time, I could leave the valley floor and ride up to the top of the mountain with no problems. Within a few days my throat was healed.

Now that my asthma was under control, Dr. Kenneth Neilson arranged for an electro-cardiologist, Dr. Nischala Nannapaneni in his office to perform an Ablation on my heart. Since November 1, 2024, after the Ablation on my heart, I am A-fib free, and my blood pressure is back to normal.

Again, I am living proof that God's love is abundant. God does listen to our prayers though our hearts. It is one thing to pray, but it is different when we pray with all your heart. Throughout this book, I have stressed that very important point. It is our job to listen to His answers and then act upon them! I had this veracity throughout my life.

Here are some Bible verses that I read daily. Some are the ones Dodie used, and I have added many more that helped me regain not only my health, but strength with the terrible political issues facing America. With these scriptures, Jim and I regained our joy.

I urge everyone to search the Bible to learn the Word of God. It contains the blueprint for healing which God wrote out for us. It's funny, now when I read and study the Bible, God's blueprints for health, happiness, success, and protection seem to jump out at me.

Jesus laid the very foundation for each of us to learn as we 'abide' with Him in the scriptures. After His death and resurrection, the apostles after receiving the Gift of The Holy Spirit continued His Ministry by boldly witnessing, teaching and spreading the Word of the Gospel to the ends of the earth.

Most of these scriptures are from the Catholic Great Adventure by Ascension Publishing, LLC. A few of the scriptures are from the King James Version and the New International Version.

Pope John Paul II wrote in the CCC his famous *Salvifici Doloris 27* concerning suffering with Christ. "Down through the centuries and generations it has been seen that in suffering, there is concealed a particular power that draws a person interiorly close to Christ, a special grace." His speech goes on to share: "The Father eternally loving the Son, and the Son eternally loving the Father, and the love between them so real, that He is a person, The Holy Spirit."

This same Gift of The Holy Spirit that Jesus left with the apostles, He also left for all generations to come, so He is always with us.

The next chapter contains the scriptures I read to reprogram my mind like Dodie Osteen, and countless others that understand the importance of reading the scriptures daily.

Chapter Twenty-One

Daily Scripture Readings

EXODUS 15:26

If you diligently heed the voice of the Lord your God and do what is right in His sight, give ear to His commandments and keep all His statues, I will put none of the diseases on you which I have brought on the Egyptians. For I am the Lord who heals you.

EXODUS 23:25

You shall serve the Lord your God, and I will bless your bread and water; and I will take sickness away from the midst of you.

DEUTERONOMY 7:15

And the Lord will take away from you all sickness; and none of the evil diseases of Egypt, which you knew, will He inflict upon you, but He will lay them upon all who hate you.

DEUTERONOMY 28:1,2

And if you obey the voice of the Lord your God, being careful to do all His commandments which I command you this day, the Lord your God will set you above all the nations of the earth. And all these blessings shall come to you and overtake you if you obey the voice of the Lord your God.

DEUTERONOMY 30:19

I call upon heaven and earth to witness against you this day, that I have set before you, life and death, blessings, and curses; therefore, choose life, that you and your descendants may live.

JOSHUA 1:9

Have I not commanded you? Be strong and courageous. Do not be terrified, do not be discouraged, for the Lord your God will be with you wherever you go.

JOSHUA 21:45

Not one of all the good promises which the Lord had made to the house of Israel had failed; all came to pass.

1 KINGS 8:56

"Blessed be the Lord who has given rest to His people Israel, according to all that He promised; not one word has failed of all His good promise, which He uttered by Moses, His servant."

2 CHRONICLES 7:14

If My people, who are called by My Name, will humble themselves and pray and seek My Face and turn from their wicked ways, then will I hear from heaven and will forgive their sins and will heal their land.

PSALMS 27:1

The LORD is my light and salvation-whom shall, I fear? The LORD is the stronghold of my life-of whom shall I be afraid?

PSALMS 46:1

God is our refuge and strength, an ever-present help in trouble.

PSALMS 20:1 (Protection)

May the Lord answer you when you are in distress; may the Name of the God of Jacob protect you.

PSALMS 55:22

Cast your cares on the LORD and He will sustain you; He will never let the righteous fall.

PSALMS 56:9 (NIV) (First line of defense.)

The day we pray, the tide of the battle turns.

PSALMS 89:34

I will not violate My covenant or alter the Word that went forth from My lips.

PSALMS 91:1-16

He that dwells in the shelter of the Most High shall abide in the shadow of The Almighty. I will say of the Lord, "He is my refuge and my fortress, my God, in whom I trust." Surely, He will save you from the fowler's snare and from the deadly pestilence. He will cover you with His feathers, and under His wings you will find refuge; His faithfulness will be your shield and rampart. You will not fear the terror of night, nor the arrow that flies by day, nor the pestilence that stalks in the darkness, nor the plague that destroys at midday. A thousand may fall at your side, ten thousand at your right hand, but it will not come near you. You will only observe with your eyes and see the punishment of the wicked. *Because you have made the Lord your refuge, the Most High your habitation, no scourge will come near your tent. For He will give His angels charge of you to guard you in all your ways. On their hands they will bear you up, lest you dash your foot against a stone. You will tread on the lion and the adder, the young lion, and the serpent you will trample under foot. "Because he clings to Me in love," says the Lord. "I will deliver him; I will protect him because he knows My Name. When he calls to Me, I will answer him; I will be with him in trouble, I will rescue him and honor him. With long life I will satisfy him and show him my Salvation."*

PSALMS 103: 1-5

Bless the Lord, O my soul; and all that is within me, bless His Holy Name! Bless the Lord, O my soul, and forget not all His benefits, who forgives your iniquities, who heals all your diseases, who redeems your life from the Pit, who crowns you with mercy and compassion, who satisfies you with good as long as you live so that your youth is renewed like the Eagle's.

PSALMS 105:37 (NIV)

He (God) also brought them out with silver and gold, and there was none feeble among His tribes.

PSALMS 107:20

He sent forth His Word, and healed them, and delivered them from destruction.

PSALMS 110:1

The Lord (God) says of my Lord (Jesus); "Sit at My Right Hand, till I make Your enemies Your footstool."

PSALMS 118:17

I shall not die, but I shall live and recount the deeds of the Lord.

PSALMS 147:3

He heals the brokenhearted and binds up their wounds.

PROVERBS 3:7,8

Be not wise in your own eyes; fear the Lord and turn away from evil. It will be healing to your flesh and refreshment to your bones.

PROVERBS 4:20-22

My son, be attentive to My Words; incline your ear to My sayings. Let them not escape from your sight; and keep them within your heart. For they are life to him who finds them, and healing to all his flesh.

PROVERBS 6:2 (Warning)

You are snared in the utterance of your lips, caught in the words of your mouth.

PROVERBS 16:9 (NIV)

"In their hearts, humans plan their course, but the Lord establishes their steps."

PROVERBS 17:22 (Health)

A cheerful heart is good medicine, but a crushed spirit dries up the bones.

PROVERBS 29:25

Fear of man will prove to be a snare, but whoever trusts in the LORD is kept safe.

ISAIAH 26:3

You will keep in perfect peace him whose mind is steadfast because he trusts in You (The Lord).

ISAIAH 40:31

But they who wait for the Lord shall renew their strength, they shall mount up with wings like the Eagles, they shall run and not be weary, they shall walk and not faint.

ISAIAH 41:10,13 (Take hold of God's right hand.)

Fear not, for I am with you, be not dismayed, for I am your God; I will strengthen you, I will help you, I will uphold you with My Victorious Right Hand. For I, the Lord your God, hold your right hand; it is I who say to you, "Fear not, I will help you."

ISAIAH 43:1,2

"But now, this is what the Lord (Jesus) says-He who created you, O Jacob, He who formed you, O Israel: '" Fear not, for I have redeemed you; I have summoned you by name, you are

Mine. When you pass through the waters, I will be with you; and when you pass through the rivers, they will not sweep over you. When you walk through the fire, you will not be burned; the flames will not set you ablaze."'

ISAIAH 43:25,26

"I, I am He who blots out your transgressions for My own sake, and I will not remember your sins. Put Me in remembrance, let us argue together; set forth your case, that you may be proved right."

ISAIAH 44:1,2

"But now hear, O Jacob My servant, Israel whom I have chosen!" Thus says the Lord who made you, who formed you from the womb, I will help you.

ISAIAH 53:5

But He (Jesus) was wounded for our transgressions, He was bruised for our iniquities; upon Him was the chastisement that made us whole, and by His stripes we are healed.

JOB 12:10

In His (Jesus) hands is the life of every creature, and the breath of all mankind.

JEREMIAH 1:5

"Before I formed you in the womb I knew you, and before you were born, I consecrated you; I appointed you a prophet to the nations."

JEREMIAH 1:12

Then the Lord said to me, "You have seen well, for I am watching over My Word to perform it."

JEREMIAH 17:7

"But blessed to the man who trusts in the Lord, whose confidence is in Him."

JEREMIAH 29:11

"For I know the plans I have for you," declares the Lord, "plans to prosper you and not to harm you, plans to give you hope and a future."

JEREMIAH 29:13

You will seek Me and find Me when you seek Me with all your heart.

JEREMIAH 30:17

"For I will restore health to you, and your wounds I will heal," says the Lord.

LAMENTATIONS 3:25

The LORD is good to those whose hope is in Him, to the ones who seeks Him.

HOSEA 4:6

My people are destroyed for lack of knowledge.

(People are sick and dying because they do not know what the scriptures teach concerning healing.)

JOEL 3:10 (NIV)
Let the weak say, "I am strong."

NAHUM 1:9 (NIV)
Affliction will not rise up a second time.

MALACHI 3:10
"Bring the full tithes into the storehouse, that there may be food in My house; and thereby put Me to the test," says the Lord of Hosts, "if I will not open the windows of heaven for you and pour down for you an overflowing blessing."

MATTHEW 4:23,24
And He (Jesus) went about all Galilee, teaching in their synagogues and preaching the Gospel of the Kingdom and healing every disease and every infirmity among the people. So, His fame spread throughout all Syria, and they brought Him all the sick, those afflicted with various diseases and pains, demoniacs, epileptics, and paralytics, and He healed them.

MATTHEW 8:1-3
When He (Jesus) came down from the mountain, great crowds followed Him; and behold, a leper came to Him and knelt before Him, saying, "Lord, if You will, You can make me clean. And He (Jesus) stretched out His hand and touched him, saying, "I will; be clean."

MATTHEW 8:16,17
That evening they brought to Him (Jesus) many who were possessed with demons; and He cast out the spirits with a

Word and healed all who were sick. This was to fulfil what was spoken by the Prophet Isaiah (53:5), "He took our infirmities and bore our diseases."

MATTHEW 9:20-22

And behold, a woman who had suffered from a hemorrhage for twelve years came up behind Him (Jesus) and touched the fringe of His garment; for she said to herself, "If I only touch His garment, I shall be made well." Jesus turned, and seeing her He said, "Take heart, daughter; your faith has made you well."

MATTHEW 9:27-30

And as Jesus passed on from there, two blind men followed Him, crying aloud, "Have mercy on us, Son of David." When He entered the house, the blind men came to Him; and Jesus said to them, "Do you believe that I am able to do this?" They said to Him, "Yes, Lord." Then He touched their eyes, saying, "According to your faith let it be done to you." And their eyes were opened.

MATTHEW 11:4,5

And Jesus answered them, "Go and tell John (The Baptist) what you hear and see: The blind receive sight, the lame walk, those who have leprosy are cured, the deaf hear, the dead are raised, and the good news is preached to the poor.

MATTHEW 18:18

Jesus tells Peter, "Truly, I say to you, whatever you bind on earth shall be bound in heaven, and whatever you loose on earth shall be loosed in heaven."

MATTHEW 18:19

"Again, I say to you, if two of you agree on earth about anything they ask, it will be done for them by My Father in heaven."

MATTHEW 18:20

"For where two or three are gathered in My Name, there am I in the midst of them."

MATTHEW 21:21,22 (We must have the faith.)

And Jesus answered them, "Truly, I say to you, if you have faith and never doubt, you will not only do what has been done to the fig tree, but even if you say to this mountain, 'Be taken up and cast into the sea,' it will be done. And whatever you ask in prayer, you will receive, if you have faith."

MARK 11:25 (Warning)

"And whenever you stand praying, forgive, if you have anything against any one; so that your Father also who is in heaven may forgive you your trespasses."

MARK 16:17,18

"And these signs will accompany those who believe; in My Name (Jesus) they will cast out demons; they will speak in new tongues, they will pick up serpents and if they drink any deadly thing, it will not hurt them; they will lay their hands on the sick, and they will recover."

LUKE 10:19

"Behold, I have given you authority to tread upon serpents and scorpions, and over all the power of the enemy: and nothing shall hurt you."

JOHN 4:25,26 (Jesus goes out of His way for His sheep.)

The woman (at the Well) said to Him, "I know the Messiah is coming, He who is called the Christ; when He comes, He will show us all things." Jesus said to her, "I who speak to you am He."

JOHN 9:31

We know that God does not listen to sinners, but if anyone is a worshiper of God and does His will, God listens to him.

JOHN 10:10

"The thief comes only to steal and kill and destroy; I (Jesus) came that they may have life and have it abundantly."

JOHN 10:11

"I am the Good Shepherd. The Good Shepherd lays down His life for the sheep."

JOHN 11:40

Then Jesus said to Lazarus' sister Martha, "Did I not tell you that if you believed, you would see the glory of God?

JOHN 16:33

"I have told you these things, so that in Me you may have peace. In this world you will have trouble. But take heart! I have overcome the world."

John 20:29

Jesus said to Thomas, "You have believed because you have seen Me. Blessed are those who have not seen and yet believe."

ROMANS 4:8

If we live, we live to the Lord; and if we die, we die to the Lord. So, whether we live or die, we belong to the Lord.

ROMANS 4:17-21

As Abraham, for he is the father of us all, as it is written, "I have made you the father of many nations" —in the presence of the God in whom he believed, who gives life to the dead and calls into existence the things that do not exist. In hope he (Abraham) believed against hope, that he should become the father of many nations; as he had been told, "So shall your descendants be." He did not weaken in Faith when he considered his own body, which was as good as dead because he was about a hundred years old, or when he considered the barrenness of Sarah's womb. No distrust made him waver concerning the promise of God, but he grew strong in his faith as he gave glory to God, fully convinced that God was able to do what He had promised.

ROMANS 8:11

If the Spirit of Him who raised Jesus from the dead dwells in you, He who raised Christ Jesus from the dead will give life to your mortal bodies also through His Sprit who dwells in you.

ROMANS 8:28

And we know that in all things God works for the good of those who love Him, who have been called according to His purpose.

1 CORINTHIANS 15:33 (Be careful who you associate with.)

Do not be deceived; "Bad company ruins good morals."

2 CORINTHIANS 10:4,5 (KJV)

For the weapons of our warfare are not carnal, but mighty through God to the pulling down of strongholds: Casting down imaginations, and every high thing that exalted itself against the knowledge of God and bringing into captivity every thought to the obedience of Christ.

GALATIONS 3:13,14

Christ redeemed us from the curse of the law, having become a curse for us—for it is written, "Cursed be everyone who hangs on a tree" —that in Christ Jesus the blessing of Abraham might come upon the Gentiles, that we might receive the promise of the Spirit through Faith

(The curse of the law of Abraham was sin, sickness, and poverty. On the cross Jesus paid the price so that we will not have to suffer them.)

Ephesians 6:10-17

Finally, be strong in the Lord and in the strength of His might. Put on the whole armor of God, that you may be able to stand against the wiles of the Devil. For we are not contending against flesh and blood, but against the principalities, against the powers, against the world rulers of this present darkness, against the spiritual hosts of wickedness in the heavenly places. Therefore, take the whole Armor of God that you may be able to withstand in the Evil Day, and having done all, to stand. Stand therefore, having fastened the belt of truth around your waist, and having put on the breastplate of righteousness, and having shod your feet with the equipment of the gospel of peace, besides all these taking the shield of Faith, with which you can quench all the flaming darts of the Evil One. And take the helmet of salvation, and the sword of the Spirit, which is the Word of God.

Philippians 2:13

For God is at work in you, both to will and to work, for His good pleasure.

Philippians 4:8

Finally, brethren, whatever is true, whatever is honorable, whatever is just, whatever is pure, whatever is lovely, whatever is gracious, if there is any excellence, if there is anything worthy of praise, think about these things. What you have learned and received and heard and seen in Me, do; and the God of peace will be with you.

1 TIMOTHY 3:4

He must manage his own family well and see that his children obey him with proper respect.

2 TIMOTHY 1:7

For God did not give us a spirit of timidity but a spirit of power, and love, and self-control.

HEBREWS 1:3,4

He (Jesus) reflects the glory of God and bears the very stamp of His nature, upholding the universe by His Word of Power. When He had made purification for sins, He sat down at the Right Hand of the Majesty on High, having become so much superior to angels and the Name He obtained is more excellent than theirs.

HEBREWS 4:12

For the Word of God is living and active, sharper than any two-edged sword, piercing to the division of soul and spirit, of joints and marrow, and discerning the thoughts and intentions of the heart.

(Jesus gave us the power of the scriptures in our daily lives for healing and protection.)

HEBREWS 10:23

Let us hold fast the confession of our hope without wavering, for He (Jesus) who promised is faithful.

HEBREWS 10:24,25 (Importance of attending church.)

And let us consider how to stir up one another to love and good works, not neglecting to meet together, as in the habit of some, but encouraging one another, and all the more as you see The Day drawing nearby.

HEBREWS 10:35

Therefore, do not throw away your confidence, which has a great reward.

HEBREWS 11:6

And without Faith it is impossible to please Him. For whoever would draw near to God must believe that He exists and that He rewards those who seek Him.

HEBREWS 11:11

By faith Sarah herself received power to conceive, even when she was past the age, since she considered Him (God) faithful who had promised.

HEBREWS 12:2

Looking to Jesus the pioneer and perfector of our faith, who for joy that was set before Him endures the cross, dispersing the shame, and is seated at the Right Hand of the Throne of God.

HEBREWS 13:8

Jesus Christ is the same yesterday, today, and forever.

(Jesus heals us today like He did when He walked upon the earth.)

HEBREWS 13:5,6 (KJV)

Let your conversation be without covetousness; and be content with such things as you have for, He (God) hath said, "I will never leave thee, nor forsake thee."

JAMES 1:5

If any of you lacks wisdom, let him ask God, who gives to all men generously and without reproaching, and it will be given him.

JAMES 3:17

But the wisdom from above is, first pure, then peaceable, gentle, open to reason, full of mercy and good fruits, without uncertainty or insincerity.

JAMES 5:14,15

Is any among you sick? Let him call for the elders of the Church, and let them pray over him, anointing him with oil in the name of the Lord; and the Lord will raise him up; and he will be forgiven of sins.

JAMES 5:16

Therefore, confess your sins to one another, and pray for one another, that you may be healed. The prayer of a righteous man has great power in its effects.

1 PETER 2:24

He (Jesus) Himself bore our sins in His body on the tree, that we might die to sin and live to righteousness. By His wounds you were healed.

(Peter stressed on the cross Jesus paid the price for all generations to come.)

1 PETER 3:22

Who (Jesus) has gone into heaven and is seated at the Right Hand of God, with angels, authorities, and powers subject to Him.

1 PETER 5:7,8

Cast all your anxieties on Him (Jesus), for He cares about you. Be sober, be watchful. Your adversary the devil prowls around like a roaring lion, seeking someone to devour. Resist him steadfast in faith.

1 JOHN 3:21,22

Beloved, if our hearts do not condemn us, we have confidence for God; and we receive from Him whatever we ask, because we keep His commandments and do what pleases Him.

1 JOHN 5:14,15

And this is the confidence which we have in Him, that if we ask anything according to His will, He hears us. And if we know that He hears us in whatever we ask, we know that we have obtained the request made of Him.

3 JOHN 1:4

I have no greater joy than to hear that my children are walking in the truth.

3 JOHN 2 (KJV)

Beloved, I wish above all things that thou mayest prosper and be in good health, even as thy soul prosperous.

REVELATIONS 12:11 (NIV)

And they overcame him by the Blood of the Lamb and by the word of their testimony.

(God wants you to give Him the glory of healing you. You are now His chosen vessel to lead others to Him.)

ST. JOHN PAUL II (From *Salvifici Doloris*)

The Trinity: the Father eternally loving the Son, and the Son eternally loving the Father, and the love between them so real, that He is a Person; the Holy Spirit.

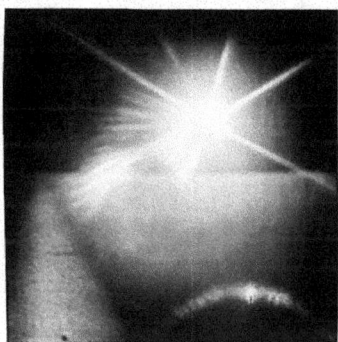

Figure #1

The ring of angels around the roof of Nancy Fowlers house.

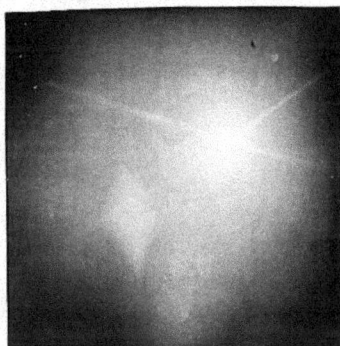

Figure #2

Mary ascending from the roof.

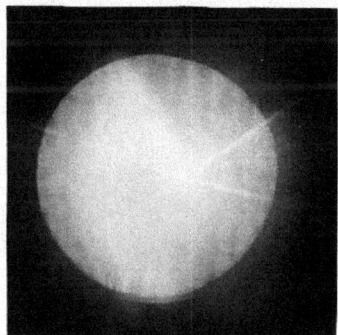

Figure #3

Mary standing through the Eucharist.

Figure #4

White marble statue of Mother Mary.

Figure #5

Statue of Jesus suffering on the cross.

www.ingramcontent.com/pod-product-compliance
Lightning Source LLC
Chambersburg PA
CBHW072346090426
42741CB00012B/2939